D0820325

PACK MY BAG

BOOKS BY HENRY GREEN

FICTION

Blindness

Living

Party Going

Caught

Loving

Back

Concluding

Nothing

Doting

NONFICTION

Pack My Bag

Surviving

Henry Green

PACK MY BAG

A Self~Portrait

Introduction by SEBASTIAN YORKE

A NEW DIRECTIONS BOOK

Manufactured in the United States of America.
New Directions Books are printed on acid-free paper.
First published clothbound by New Directions in 1993.

The Publishers thank The Estate of Henry Yorke and The Peters, Fraser and Dunlop Group Ltd. for permission to reproduce the letter from Evelyn Waugh to Henry Green in the introduction to this edition.

Library of Congress Cataloging-in-Publication Data
Green, Henry, 1905-1974.
    Pack my bag : a self-portrait / Henry Green.
    p. cm.
    ISBN 0-8112-1234-3
    1. Green, Henry, 1905-1974—Biography—Youth.   2. Novelists,
English—20th century—Biography.   I. Title.
PR6013.R416Z465   1993   92-39386
823'.912—dc20   CIP

New Directions Books are published for James Laughlin
by New Directions Publishing Corporation
80 Eighth Avenue, New York 10011

INTRODUCTION

Pack My Bag is a mid-term autobiography written by Henry Green, my father, at the age of thirty-three. It was published in 1940 when he was just beginning to get himself established as a novelist, having already published, with some difficulty, three books of fiction: *Blindness, Living*, and *Party Going*. After *Blindness* he had also started, but had been unable to finish, another novel called *Mood*. To his disappointment, the last novel, *Party Going*, which had taken eight years to write, had been rejected by his publishers, Dents, and accepted by Leonard and Virginia Woolf, only after strong representations from Goronwy Rees and John Lehmann, for publication at their Hogarth Press. In 1938 he became convinced that there would be another terrible war and moreover, having vivid schoolboy memories of the carnage of the First World War, that he was sure to die in it himself. The book entitled *Pack My Bag*, which were the last words uttered by the philosopher Bradley on his death bed, was born out of this morbid anxiety. Happily the outcome of the Second World

War, for Henry Green at least, was to be less dramatic. He would survive it unscathed except, as he constantly reminded his friends, for *"untold"* damage to his hearing and stomach, write another six novels—two of these during that same war—and live on quietly for a further thirty-five years in Knightsbridge, London.

Henry Green's real name was Henry Yorke and he was the younger of two surviving sons of a family who lived in a large and imposing house in Gloucestershire, set in a 2500 acre estate beside the River Severn. The family had aristocratic roots and, on the male side, a strong leaning towards classical scholarship. His mother, who came from a titled and landed family in Sussex, was a remarkable figure. To her eldest grandson, she was all warmth and affection, but first appearances were disconcerting. Born with a curvature of the spine, her frame was small and bent, and generally she would dress in black or dark navy blue with a hat and a feather drawn well down over her eyes. On formal occasions a dyed fur stole mounted with the mask of a snarling fox would be slung over one shoulder. Her speech was blunt and clipped in military style. In her younger days she had been an avid sportswoman, hunting furiously, breeding racehorses from a stallion called White Knight, and shooting pheasants with a specially adapted twenty bore shotgun. In her old age, adamantly opposed to dentures, she was reduced to one tooth, stained brown because she chainsmoked Turkish cigarettes. But underneath this forbidding exterior, there was an active mind with a genuine fascination for people of all classes. Despite the lack of any formal education, she read voraciously (never novels), but above all she loved to gossip and talk, and she possessed an unique wit. It was said that she could more than hold her own in witty conversation with her son's friends, such as Maurice Bowra and John Sparrow, who visited the house when he was up at Oxford. Henry's father, who had no inherited wealth, ran the family engineering firm which had been bought for him by his father, and pursued a parallel City career in banking and insurance; a reserved and aloof figure, difficult to communicate with, he was in Birmingham and London during the week and back in Gloucestershire for long weekends where he attended to matters on his estate. He was humourless, and somewhat jealous of his wife's popularity, was wont to tease and bully her in heavy-handed, but harmless fashion. Their principal recreation was hunting and other field sports. The sons, who were close in their youth, but who grew apart later, were uneasy participants in the sporting life their parents led. Henry, who was less sociable than his brother, preferred the more solitary pursuits of billiards and fly fishing.

Pack My Bag is his account of what he observed and felt while growing up in those surroundings and attending two *"fashionable"* boarding schools and university. There are also descriptions in the book of the short period he spent in France with cousins learning the language and, briefly, of the two year period when he served his apprenticeship in his father's Birmingham factory and wrote his second novel, *Living*. This privileged up-bringing, with which he never seems uncomfortable in the book, must have been typical of others of his generation, but it was a background which, in later life, he went to considerable lengths to play down or even suppress.

Written between 1938–39, the book in fact only covers the first twenty-four years of his life, from his birth in 1905 to 1929, and it ends tenderly with the words referring to his marriage to my mother in that year *". . . there was love"*. Nothing is said about the nine years that followed his marriage when my parents, a handsome couple much in demand by the smart set, settled in London and lived the lives of Bright Young Things about town. More surprisingly, perhaps, nothing at all is said in the book about his school friends or university contemporaries. However, truer to his style, there are memorable studies of his mother's gardener, the headmaster and gym instructor from his first school as well as fleeting glimpses of the maids from his schools, Dotty Boo and Dinge. Accounts of his two schools and university occupy at least half of the book but he does not identify them by name, although it becomes obvious that the main school is Eton College and the university, Oxford. These omissions mystified and irritated his contemporary, Evelyn Waugh, who liked the book but wrote critically, *"I read it [with] increasing delight. It got better and better, I thought, towards the end. I never tire of hearing you talk about women and I wish there had been very much more indeed about them and the extraordinary things they say. Thank you by the way for 'Charlies', an entirely new word to me. I wish there had been twice as much about Oxford, four times as much about Hunt Balls, twice as much about the factory. Only one thing disconcerted me—more in this book than any of the novels. The proletarian grammar—the 'likes' for 'ases', the 'bikes' for 'bicycles', 'hims' for 'hes', etc. and then the sudden resumption of gentleman's language whenever you write of sport. And I thought the school 'down the river' a pity as tho' you hadn't got over snobbery. Both these things upset me—school 'by the river' and the correct hunting terms. But it was a book no-one else could have written and it makes me feel I know [you] far less well than I did before which, in a way, I take to be its purpose."*

There is indeed a feeling about the book that he was in a hurry to write it and get it out of the way quickly, after all the problems with his third novel, *Party Going.* One senses that he wanted to be free of his past, free to gear himself up for the war—while he was writing it he was training to be an auxiliary fireman in London—and free to concentrate on a new novel about the impending war. The first part reads more fluently than the last, which is somewhat uneven, suggesting that he finished it in a hurried fashion. Certainly this was the view of his new publisher, John Lehmann, who asked him to *"rework"* the later part. And it is possible now to see more clearly that the book did indeed mark something of a turning-point in his life. Having got it off his chest, he was soon swallowed up in the London blitz, where he served as an ordinary fireman manning a Dual Purpose (DP) pump. He moved to a smaller house, forsook the fashionable life and began to cut himself off from his family and old friends to plough his independent furrow in the boardroom and pub rather than the literary salon and smart cocktail party.

A difficulty of any mid-term autobiography must be what can or cannot be said about close relations, in his case his parents who were still living. This was a problem made no easier by their attitudes towards his books. His father regarded them with silent contempt because they did not make money, and his mother never tried to disguise the fact that she did not understand them at all. *"Are Henry's books* any good, *dear?"* was a question constantly asked of her grandson. Further, on at least one occasion in the thirties, when he and his father were working together in the family engineering business, Henry had walked out of the office in a rage at his father's meanness, and by all accounts he was already beginning to distance himself from his mother (which was difficult because she was socially demanding and not easily put off). Yet in the book he writes touchingly of his parents, *". . . I believe we were never far from each other's thoughts. I do not suppose a day has passed when I have not thought of them . . ."*. He sent the typescript to her with a carefully drafted letter inviting her to *"object to any purely family reference in it"* and he added *"I am too near it to know whether you will like it or not. But as far as I am concerned it is true."* Her letter of reply, if one was sent, does not survive, but her typescript corrections do. She suggested eight corrections, of which the only really important one to her was that concerning his housemaster at Eton College. Henry had written *"But I think he hated me and I knew I hated him and I still do. He is the one man I would gladly trip up if I saw him run, though I would only do it if he was not looking."* Had he put this in to tease her? She responded with a savage *"omit this"* against the second sentence. He did so dutifully, and he also removed the words *"and I still do"* from the first sentence. Of the remaining seven corrections none were of great substance; one involved her own father. Henry had written up in extravagant fashion a story which must have been part of the family mythology: *"My mother's father I believe went out [hunting] with a servant who carried two axes in his saddle and because there was so much wire in his country (they were his own hounds) every variety of wire clipper as well and yet he saw as much as anyone of what went on. Those who, galloping hard and jumping everything, were seldom out of sight of hounds were seldom out of earshot of his voice encouraging his man as he chopped the fences down, for my grandfather had lost his nerve and would not jump. After hunting so they say he would go out in his pink coat, still in his boots and play golf in the park with his butler in a bowler hat carrying the clubs."* Her correction reads *"he* always *carried his own clubs"*. Perhaps she could still picture the bizarre scene in her mind's eye, but it was typical of her to come down hard on so unexpected and inconsequential a detail.

Significantly none of these seven suggested corrections were adopted in the published version—perhaps he was confident she would not re-read the book with any care.

Of all the vivid images of his childhood and adolescence brought to life in the book—the Hunt Balls, the Bump suppers, the fishing—the most arresting and magical describes the shell-shocked soldiers who were billeted at the family home during the First World War, when, much to the delight of his mother who loved to gossip every morning with the local district nurse, the house was turned into a convalescent home for Army and Air Force Officers. (The latter were quickly banned from the hospital because they were uncontrollable). It was a hospital without anaesthetics or the familiar whiff of disinfectant in the corridors, but an atmosphere of doom pervades his descriptions of this rackety enterprise. The patients were half-crazed—if they recovered they would be sent back to the front and almost certainly, as officers, machine-gunned to death by the Hun. They are observed in coldly clinical fashion but described with much tenderness and understanding. The account of the bicycle ride to Chacely Church with one of these officers is particularly memorable. These unfortunate men must have made a deep impression on a schoolboy of eleven or twelve back from boarding school for his holidays. And it is tempting to think that all the black humour that came out much later in my father's talk though never in his books—the wild stories about dentists, amputees and collisions at sea and so on—must in some way be linked to these wounded soldiers.

By contemporary accounts the book was not well received in the family and my father, for his own private reasons, chose to visit the family home rarely, if ever again.

But for his son, who by his choice spent every school holiday in the same house with his grandparents, there are many moments in reading the book when the skin crawls and he wants to shout *"I was there too!"*

Sebastian Yorke, Leeds, 1992

I WAS born a mouthbreather with a silver spoon in 1905, three years after one war and nine before another, too late for both. But not too late for the war which seems to be coming upon us now and that is a reason to put down what comes to mind before one is killed, and surely it would be asking much to pretend one had a chance to live.

That is my excuse, that we who may not have time to write anything else must do what we now can. If we have no time to chew another book over we must turn to what comes first to mind and that must be how one changed from boy to man, how one lived, things and people and one's attitude. All of these otherwise would be used in novels, material is better in that form or in any other that is not directly personal, but we I feel no longer have the time. We should be taking stock.

Most things boil down to people, or at least most houses to those who live in them, so Forthampton boils down to Poole, who did not live in but was gardener about the place for years. He used to lean on his spade with one foot up and go to sleep very much as later one was to see friends lean up against

I

bars and go to sleep with one foot on the rail. In his quietness and with his beard he was fascinating to a child and I was always running out to him. He did not like my mother and when he was awake, which was not often, it was mostly against her that he talked. Was this the first disloyalty that I listened to him and did my brothers walk away while I stayed? I only know that I adored her and that nothing he said began to alter this even; it was as though someone were bringing out mean things about adoration to another full of his first love, what was said came as laughter in the face of creation and this and my love for my mother is what I first remember.

The house was called Forthampton Cottage and, like so many names of country houses, it is misleading. Here was no cottage and round and about was the English garden, flower beds surrounding a number of small lawns. The house, washed over in pink, was built raised up above these lawns on a low embankment, and it troubled Poole to mow the sides, he had a bad leg. Next to the house close to our nursery windows a huge beech tree grew, resplendent and vast, with millions of spiders. In that embankment was the coal cellar door, a wooden frame covered with wirenetting, and when I had discovered it and went to warn Poole it was there so full of treasure and menaces, he said he had always known. I suppose he had not much use for children.

We lived here in the early years, in soft lands and climate influenced by the Severn, until my grandfather died and we moved to the big house a mile nearer the river where it went along below the garden. Poole retired when this change came. And in this new house, Forthampton Court, we could see Tewkesbury Abbey from the lawn. Where from the Cottage we could only hear its bells when the wind was right, here they were much nearer, only over the river, and always at any time the pealing bells would throw their tumbling drifting noise under thick steaming August hours and over meadows between, laying up a nostalgia in after years for evenings at home.

Poole, so they say, could never forgive my mother when soon after marriage she made him bowl mangel wurzels across one lawn for her to shoot at. I see her better after she had put the gun away, when she would come out as she still does with her retriever and a long hooked stick and all day would stand some way off with it raised on high, threatening the dog. Not one of her many dogs obeyed one of her commands. But in those days they say she used to call out, " Gardener, gardener, I'm going to shoot! " and it was for him then clumsily to bowl them. She called him gardener it is said but I know she called him Poole.

Most people remember very little of when they were small and what small part of this time there

is that stays is coloured it is only fair to say, coloured
and readjusted until the picture which was there,
what does come back, has been over-painted and
retouched enough to make it an unreliable account
of what used to be. But while this presentation is
inaccurate and so can no longer be called a movie,
or a set of stills, it does gain by what it is not, or, in
other words, it does set out what seems to have gone
on; that is it gives, as far as such things can and as
far as they can be interesting, what one thinks has
gone to make one up.

If I say I remember, as it seems to me I do, one of
the maids, that poor thing whose breath smelled,
come in one morning to tell us the *Titanic* had gone
down, it may be that much later they had told me
I should have remembered at the age I was then
and that their saying this had suggested I did
remember. But I do know, and they would not,
that her breath was bad, that when she knelt down
to do one up in front it was all one could manage to
stand there. But I never said so, I think, although I
remember asking our head housemaid why she had
a moustache. She did not seem to mind but I had
been overheard and the others did. Why one and
not the other when at that age moustache and bad
breath were all the same, things which they had ?

She used to stand, the younger one that is, at one
end of the nursery passage and I would run and
jump for her to lift me over her head. When she

put me down again it always jarred but I never told them and used to beg for more, the just once more again.

There were windows in this passage which looked out on to a corridor open to the sky between pantries and kitchens and all the back wall of our stables. Along it was heaped, each in a bin, cinders, refuse of all kinds, empty tins and clinkers sprinkled all of them with wet exhausted tea leaves dumped on top, with their smell. I suppose she was looking out for the groom but if I ever catch that smell in back-yards my heels begin to ache as they did then, so to speak, but it is my toes hurt now.

One could not have enough sugar in those days and there were times as in every nursery, is my son allowed to do it ? when we could make toffee under the nanny's eye. Why can I hardly remember her ? Only once at all clearly and then she was sick after eating fish much later when we were in the second house in London. Later still when she was dead my father told me it was in part my fault for giving her so much to do. I was innocent and cried. I can't have thought of her for twenty years. What was she like and did she ever speak to Poole ?

Why is it, too, that one loved jumping to that nursemaid and hated it not six years later when in the gym at my first school they made us jump from a board over a leather horse into the arms of the sergeant major ? Sex you say, but then there was her breath and I can't think sex meant so much to us then.

There was the butler with his outfit of gold teeth and one black one whistling through his pantry window. He got into trouble through teaching one of my brothers how to smoke and had to go, much like some maids teach little boys to kiss they say but not in my experience. I saw him once more after he left. It was during the war at my first school when we were on one of our Sunday walks and so was he. He was dressed as a private and it was painful to both of us, each being some kind of prisoner. I dropped out of our crocodile and we had two embarrassed words. I remember he did not call me sir and that I blamed him for it.

And there was Lydia, one of my great grandmother's maids, the last who could remember her. She lived in one of a row of cottages below that lawn my mother had used Poole to shoot. She was like any old pensioned Russian servant in their novels of sixty years ago. Of course her cottage was very clean. I used to visit her every Sunday afternoon and she treated me with respect, so precious to little boys. She was prehistoric, wore starched white bonnets and, as country people will, the fashions of a hundred years ago. If anyone idly says what were people like then let him get out into the country and anyone over seventy will show him in his talk. In fact much of their speech was fantastic and my

father, an amateur of it, was always consulting his
Dialect Dictionary. Sometimes he was able to use
a word of theirs as once, when describing an exact
kind of dryness in a pear, he brought out an Eliza-
bethan word acquired by listening over years. He
was at once corrected with a Saxon monosyllable he
had never heard and quickly making his way home
he turned this up to find it meant a drier state of
dryness.

Beyond this row of cottages where Lydia lived was
a wood called Volter's. The woods on this estate
have pretty names, Sarn Hill, Volter's, Downend,
Agborough, The Grove and not so pretty The
Allotments. Alongside Volter's a path ran to the
main road and once an old lady coming back at
night slipped and broke her leg. My mother when
she opened her window before getting into bed
heard her crying, each thin scream regularly timed,
and thought it so like a creaking wheel they had not
oiled she did no more and there that woman lay all
night, no one paying attention, perhaps no one else
used to open their windows. If they never did the
reason was probably the malaria my grandfather
could remember not far away on Longdon Marsh
when those who lived there before it was drained
shook when the fit was on them like frightened
prisoners.

Is it presumptuous to write about oneself and is
that why it is easier to write about what one has

been told when it has no bearing on what one has experienced ? Is it fair to expect people to be interested if it is boring and hard work to put down and probably so dull to read. It may be worth doing if there are others interested in all sorts of people, interested enough that is to read any sort of person's life which is not made up of running away to sea or of privations. So everything must go down that one can remember, all one's tool box, one's packet of Wrigley's, coloured by its having been used in conversation or by one's having thought of whatever it may be so many times but necessarily truer to oneself for that reason and therefore unattractive no doubt, thick with one's spittle.

How unattractive is one now, and was one more or less so then ? All I know is that I was very much alone, that is my brothers were older and the country more remote in those days of unreliable cars so that there was not much company. This meant aping one's elders before one was of an age and, in consequence, trouble and tears at home until they were glad enough to send me to school at six and three quarters and I was keen enough to go. But before that happened there are still some things to put down although there seem to be, I don't know why, surprisingly few.

There was my grandfather whom I can remember only twice, once when we met on one of his walks and he gave me a tip and I was so struck by his long white beard, and again at the end of his life when we came across him on the village green poking the bits of paper he found lying there into the ground with his stick. He liked everything to be tidy and they say that when he went to bed he used to wash his beard in rose water and then put it in a bag with two flaps to go over his ears. Or is this the sort of thing they tell children to please them ?

It was about now they gave me a blue Persian kitten which I could never leave alone. We were never separated, she was not allowed to roam at night and to the day I went to school she would follow on our walks slightly behind or at the side, making out she was hunting us or lying down to take a rest but for all the elaborate attempts she made to show no interest, never letting us out of her sight. It was not unlike taking out a film star in London, she was unwilling but she agreed to come and part of the delight she gave lay in my having been told a thing of this kind was rare so that I thought I might be an animal charmer.

When we went out we would go along Bishop's Walk or Nabletts Lane, it might be as far as Long Green.

We were well brought up and saw our parents twice a day, that is to say my father worked in London through the week and we only saw him at week-ends. We came down to their breakfast; my mother said " chairs boys " and we sat on these back against

the wall and did not talk. Then in the evening, after
my brothers had gone to school, I used to come down
alone from five to six and each time hoped they
would not hear the clock strike bed time. My
mother used to say " how much do you love me—
more than toffee ? " or " more than this much "
putting her thumb and forefinger so close together
you could hardly see between. Years later a girl
said and did the same and I could not tell her what
she had made me remember, it spoilt the moment
because I laughed. One is always laughing in
wrong places or worse, as one gets older one is
inclined to belch, it comes from pipe smoking.
There is no escape from the ridiculous or from what
has been so nice. What has been enjoyed so much so
many years ago will lie in wait to crop up again at
any time. If you once wet your bed, as I used to,
then all your life you will get up in the night. But
I cannot think of anything else, I was not left-
handed and made to use my right so that I stutter
now. I was perhaps unnaturally shy of girls for some
time, having no sisters, but that is so with every
Englishman judged by European standards. I was
perhaps shyer than most Englishmen but that only
made it the more fun later when that shyness had
worn off. I was lonely, there was not much company
of my own age, so that I was not sorry to go to school.
These things apart I can't think of anything else
although we are warned that what happened in those

days, like the wilder wild animals, lies in wait, in ambush for when one has grown up. So they say, but it never does. It was all what I take to be rich and comfortable, some months in London of which I remember nothing and the others down at home of which I remember, as you have seen, hardly anything at all.

THE school they sent me to, the private school so called, stood on a high hill in Kent and was of sharp red brick. Over its walls grew one of those creepers with leaves that turn to raw copper sheet and along the drive fir trees were planted, dark green and grey. It had been built and laid out as a school not long before so that the trees planted round its playing fields had not grown much and the windows downstairs looked to be what they were, classroom windows and upstairs those to the dormitories. The chapel stood apart with white stone facings. Inside the seats were in pitch pine varnished a bright yellow like sheet brass, with terrible grains surging over the surfaces, coming through a purple colour. There were seventy-five of us and we could just fit in.

If it is permissible to say a school is good then this was a good school although fantastic things went on particularly after the war had started. It was owned, directed, and the boys were taught all by one remarkable old man of a violent appearance. There were, of course, other masters and during the war mistresses, but these seemed hardly to exist, there

was only one who roared and seemed to be everywhere at once. He had more authority than anyone
I have met.

The boys were mostly sons of officers and there
was one peer. The first day of term we were sum-
moned to the main classroom and told this boy was
going to arrive, that he was a lord and that in spite
of this we were to treat him as one of ourselves. In
this way and at once we were introduced to the
snobbery amongst other things which make school
life, paradoxically, a larger picture, an enlargement
of the relationships which obtain between people in
the world. What I mean is that any average person
who in after-life does not go out looking for strange
characters will find truer friendship, more genuine
companionship, and conversely purer types, more
perfect examples of liars, thieves and crooks in his
first school during the six years he spends there than
he will come across in twenty years of living in
London, the kind of escaped prisoners we then are
after our education has done with us.

This is not to say the school was worse than another,
only that nothing better could be expected where
boys, fresh from the oriental intrigues and power
politics of their nurseries, were put into a strange
environment on the first occasion, in many cases,
they had left home. We came new boys into a
strange society and found not only recognized
snobbery of rank but of age as well, being older made

a difference as we were soon to find, and being good at games; also, and at this school only, perhaps, of being good at work.

Gym, carpentry, gardening, drill, in everything but music, for he would have no truck with this, Latin, Maths, in French, in history, in being a Boy Scout, there was one man and one alone to say if you were doing well at one or the other and he was our headmaster. He settled everything, he picked the sides, he tied our right legs down and bowled at them and praised the boy who, seeing he could not make a catch, put his face in the way and broke his nose. And so it was only to be expected that in circumstances such as these we lived at a higher pitch and reacted more strangely than we do now in a less competitive world where we just try to keep alive.

The food was bad and during the war it was uneatable but our headmaster's wife, who used to read the postcards we were made to write home on Sundays, could not be blamed for that in those days of rationing. If she found any comment on what we had to eat we were told we had been impolite.

As to food I was satisfactory to this extent that, being very fat at that time, so fat my parents had had the doctor in and the headmaster did the same as soon as he saw me, I became an advertisement for their cooking and would be beckoned up to be examined by inspecting parents, to be thumped and fingered like fat stock at a show. He was too clever to say my size was due to his table what he said was, " Well, this little nipper seems to get on all right," putting me under the rare summer of his smile.

Of my two brothers the eldest had been here and had gone on with a scholarship by the time I arrived, the best they had collected yet. In consequence great things were expected of me, it was important for them to have boys who won plums of that kind. I was precocious and was thought to be well advanced. My grandfather had been able to read Homer in the original when he was seven, my father at that age had done much the same, and I, all I had done was to get through all Captain Marryat by then which shows how times have changed. But they had great hopes and took me to see my brother's name in large gold letters on the scholarship board. Everything was lovely until they found I was not even up to the standard of these days, and then the old tyrant did not speak to me for seven months as though I had stolen from him. But that was later.

Each boy had a locker which was in the main classroom and had no door to it in which he had to keep his schoolbooks. Theft was made easy by this arrangement and although punished by our being made to wear coloured buttonholes, one colour meaning I am a thief another something else, we

15

became too tough to be deterred but never so much so that, when they found us out, we did not cry hysterically as tougher criminals do.

Your book was stolen, you would be punished in class if you did not have it, they caned our hands, and if you borrowed someone else's book and were found out they made you wear your buttonhole. Anything in these lockers was considered common property if no one was looking, so we took our choice of punishments.

Then each boy had his wooden chest in the gymnasium and that was where we kept cricket bats, pads, boots and anything of that kind we had of our own. Borrowing from one of these was more serious, we even regarded it as theft ourselves.

Then there was another chest which each boy had by his bed and it held his clothes. It was supposed to be sacred for we used to store our letters from home amongst the socks and pants. There was less chance of someone looking in because rules had been made against going up to the dormitories out of hours so that if anyone raided them we were there to put up a defence if we thought it worth while. No locks of any kind were allowed, as certain prisoners are not allowed shoe-laces so they dared not give us privacy, and we had those secrets of tenderness in our parents' letters always, those darlings, those kisses at the end for stronger boys to drag out by force. But there was not much rape of letters. For one thing anyone caught at a bedside might be lectured in front of the whole school and then be hated by everyone, for another we were all equally involved, we all had those who loved us at home. In that way perhaps we were not so much of a mirror to the outside world where to have someone love you is a matter of pride or of congratulation but at school it was common that we should so be loved and we were ashamed or rather did not like to show how much we felt. In many other ways we were the world in miniature for, if we were too young to have more complicated feelings than of home-sickness, gaiety and fear, our actions, and our world was one of action, were spied on just as now our feelings are objects of untold curiosity to those around us, especially to women.

When we left our nurseries, and the gardens or lumber-room we could hide in we found at school no corner even in the fields where we could be alone without having transgressed by being there and that was something we were too afraid to do at first. We were almost prisoners from ourselves and were told, a little later on perhaps, there were no thoughts or feelings we ought to have which we could not share and that if there were things we could not say then it was a crime. And so it became criminal to be afraid. And so it will be again, quite soon now I suppose.

Going to boarding-school is the biggest change one

could have, nothing can ever so estrange a nursery boy from himself. There can be nothing so alien as to join a society of seventy-five others before one is old enough to know one's mind, or rather before one has any mind at all. We were not of course allowed to have great friends, to see one boy more than another, and when later the fashion was to walk arm in arm we were told if we did this again we should be made to wear buttonholes which meant I am a little girl, or petticoats. At first it was hard to know how far one could go or in other words what rules it was popular to break, for to be punished for an unpopular crime meant ostracism and that was appalling. But in our outlook on generalities, on ideals, etcetera, we were taught to see things as our headmaster did and he saw them upside down. In my case it has been a long and in the end successful struggle to drive out what they taught me there and afterwards. A private school is a fascist state and so are public schools. Their corporate doctrines teach one ugly sides and it is when one has forgotten to be as they taught that the experience begins to be worth while.

Before coming to this place my parents had sent me to a day school so that it was not entirely strange to be in class or to play games organized by masters, that is with no cheating. Once every week in London we went by bus from somewhere behind Selfridges out to a vast expanse under Wormwood

Scrubs and played cricket under high stone walls. Here I was bullied. Fresh and worldly wise from my nursery I sneaked and got away with it. But then every evening we all of us went back home, to no dormitories then with tears at night but back to our own beds.

It had been dull at home and I was not sorry to go to school but when I got there and was shown my bed and then was taken down to tea, I knew that longing to be back as I was before I came which so works on the old, they say, in Russia that they have given up trying to win them over but wait for them to die, concentrating on the young instead. Here tea was the favourite meal and we found everyone massed round a closed door out of the main classroom. A bell was to be rung when they were ready for us. It rang and the door being flung open everyone rushed through and ran fighting down a long corridor. Too sick with strangeness to be hungry we ran to be like the others, eight or nine new boys coming last where we belonged to sit, as was right, away where we should be served last and at that by a maid with no hair, not even eyebrows at a time when these were not painted in. She wore a wig which did not fit. She was called Dotty Boo.

We sat at two long tables, seventy-five of us, and at the end drawn up to a table of his own our headmaster got down to his tea with his wife. While he was present the noise of talking was subdued, a hum, but how strange that was to us fresh from the cloistered gentility of a nursery tea, left hand on one's lap and the other putting not too much in at a time. When he was gone the older boys leant forward to look along to where we sat. They laughed. But this experience did one thing, it made it easier for us to leave home again. If they say that going to any public school makes a boy able to walk into crowded rooms some part of this is due to his having learned how to look like an old lag in earlier days. There are terms of imprisonment and terms even at kinder-gartens.

He sat beyond lowering his huge grey head to his moustache cup, thick-set with huge shoulders, always dressed in iron grey and then, lowering the cup again, he would suck at his moustaches and glare round behind those twice thick spectacles which, catching in the light, made it seem as though you had looked straight through his head to the white sky.

His eyes were so light they almost had no colour, his spectacles enlarged them to twice their size, but when he took these off to clean the glasses you saw he was old and tired, his spectacles had drilled his eyes back into his skull. Without them he was helpless. We came to know it was his spectacles which armed him. When he took them off in class, and this with him was a sign of discouragement, everyone sat back and relaxed. When he put them back he would start off again in a shout, " you little beasts . . ."

Little beasts we were, so dirty they had to search behind our ears each day and so small, as comes out in the photographs, that on looking back to what one remembers one sees it all much larger than it was. The main classroom seems immense, the masters giants and of course our headmaster, and I remember when visiting him some years later I was struck by how small he was, a heroic man, colossal figure. It is natural that we should measure everything by our own size and probably it is true that all of what is left of those days in our minds is distorted by lack of experience at that time, that is to say by the lack of any standard of comparison. Accordingly as we sat down to lessons in rows we were alive to anything which seemed strange, ready to giggle at anything we did not understand. He had to shout to keep our attention because we were always off one way or another. It is at that age if ever that one is fancy-free because little boys hardly ever think about themselves as everyone else does all the time. He may now at this distance seem harsh and bad-tempered. But he taught us more than all the others and most of what we learned was not book-learning. Even if he had appalling views on life and on how one should try to live at least he was positive, there was something to cling to, to unlearn later on.

He began by striking terror, then when we had

learned his ways so as to avoid his worst outbursts, we respected him until in my case at least I went further and came to reverence him. It was not the fault of what he taught but of his personality. It led to every kind of trick by which we hoped to catch his attention, made us curry favour fawning like little dogs that never can do wrong until we moved in a world we had made for ourselves of absurd righteousness. When, during the holidays, one of my brothers said I was lying I screamed and hit out saying over and over I never could till I can remember now the look came over his face so much as to say " my God you're hopeless! "

Back in nursery days there had been a storm and through that long window across one wall the green leaves of our beech tree had gone darker and deeper against dark clouds massing behind. We were sitting at our tea and it grew so black we wondered I remember if we should have the oil lamps lit. Those leaves dimmed in our eyes as though the sap had turned thick, they seemed to draw together against what was before us, and then the flash of lightning came with that roll of the drums and crash of all the cymbals in heaven and, as the lightning seemed to strike on the window panes to light us for the last time, I really did believe I had seen God.

Before this I had had dreams of Jesus as he is shown in popular pictures with a look of kindness on his face and I was not at all afraid and spoke to him. Each time he was going to answer when I woke up. He had been walking in our garden dressed in traditional clothes. So that when the storm burst directly over us I was sure this stroke was God and remained sure of it until I was twelve years old. To give some idea, here is one of my sermons written at that time. It is curious to notice how one's style has changed, that thirty years after one should write so differently, possibly not so well:

Brethren you know the time Jesus told Peter that he would deny him thrice and then the cock would crow and I expect you remember how Peter did deny that he had been with Jesus and how after three times denying of having been with Jesus the cock crew and how he went out and wept. Now Brethren to be frank I think that it did Peter a great deal of good for he was a very weak man. I think it hardened him for sorrow some great sorrow generally hardens a person's heart and prepares him for more bad things to come, it hardened him for the long endurance of preaching to all the heathen races and baptising them. But he was not altogether cured for when they searched to crucify him he ran away and as he was travelling along a road he saw a vision of Jesus, and Peter asked Jesus what he was going to do Jesus said: " I am going to be crucified for you " and Peter stopped Jesus and said he would go. Brethren, I think that shows that Peter was still rather weak not that I should not run away for probably I should though I must admit it needs a very strong mental brain to stop in a town where you knew you were going to be crucified in about a week's time but still it does show a weakness in faith and in mental power. Now let us turn to Jesus who had come down in order to be crucified for Peter what power of mental brain he had. Now Brethren let me describe the cross as the right path for Peter to take otherwise the thing he knew was right to do and the devil on the other side showing what pains he would have to bear and how nice it would be to run away out of the town and preach in another, so he had a veritable battle between good and evil but alas brethren evil got the better of him and he ran away. Then Our Lord came and offered to be crucified for him showing his wonderful love for Peter not only for Peter but for the whole world, but Peter could not bear to see his Lord be crucified so he went back saying he was not fit to be crucified head up so he was crucified head downwards. Now Brethren always try and do what Peter did after he saw Our Lord going to be crucified for him and conquer evil not that any one of us will be but I mean conquer your evil thoughts and always try to do what you know is right.

I print this sermon here to explain why in the school chapel I would frown at any boy who smiled, why I prayed as I did then, why, being careful in everything I did, I was so content that, when the headmaster smiled on me as he continued to do while he thought I might get the scholarship, I went on as though his recognition was no more than deserved.

It is awkward to think how terrible we must have been for I was not the only one, not in that school at any rate. We all ran to get favours from him, we would run all day. He was so all-powerful it was a form of self-protection. In his presence we were small mirrors changing in colour to the hues of his moods. It was only when he was not there that we were more like other little boys, or more like what little boys ought to be, unseen but heard.

We were always watched except at night. When we went upstairs we had so many minutes before lights out and stealing into bed we would get the last letter out again to read. We all did this. Home seemed a heaven and that we were cast out and seventy-five little boys when there was no more light lifted those lids to hide their letters back amongst their clothes and turning over went to sleep at once in the arms of whoever it was they had who loved them wherever the place was they called home.

GYM was harrowing. First of all our instructor, an army man, had so little importance it was not worth while to be in his good books. Then we were made to climb ropes and if out of curiosity we managed to get up to the top just once it was so high in proportion to our size we turned giddy. Of course there were some who did well but there was no real competition because our instructor was not the headmaster.

Parallel bars were easier but the leather horse with its jumping-board was the useless torture one is put through in fascist states or in ours when we prepare to fight those states. It used to affect me so I always had to hold up my hand.

Those lavatories were indescribable. There were no locks or bolts of course. They were cubicles in two rows and fresh from the tiled gentility at home with choice little books at hand, that shallow bowl handily by with a paperweight, our astonished senses took in what came of these cubicles all being occupied and we blinked at drawings or verses on the varnished yellow wooden walls. I wish I knew now what was written up, nothing indecent to be

sure, we were too young, just innocent comments
but how strange at first. It served at any rate to
escape the horse and later one came to regard it as
a refuge for even if one could not lock the door
custom demanded one should not be too much
disturbed.

Boxing was more fun either because little boys do
not hit too hard or because the gloves we wore were
such pillowcases no damage could be done. Also
the instructor let one try to hit him while every now
and then he would let himself be hit to show what
sort of a man he was. If a boy cried out when
punched he would say that never hurt, you hit me
like you hit him, it won't so much as make me blink.
But on that leather horse, or so it seemed to me, one
could do oneself serious injury as once in a way one
was dropped.

Next door was a small shed in which we were
allowed to keep caterpillars. We made boxes for
them in the carpenter's shop with glass fronts and
air-holes, then we bought the eggs or chrysalis from
shops that sell such things. Richer boys bought
rarer examples and when it was time and this
fantastic life came out we were kept busy getting
leaves to feed them, taking care these were dry or
they would get diarrhœa and if they did they died.
Then when they were ready to become cocoons
we would be getting sawdust for some kinds so they
might spin their spittle into sawdust bags cemented

27

hard. We never had lectures about them. They were pleasure unalloyed.

Again they let us cut laurel up to mix with water in jam jars and this let off fumes to gas any butterfly we caught. It was thought less cruel to use gas than to stick them on pins. Our difference is, now we are older, we may die both ways at one time.

We had a sorry crew of masters. There was a public beating once for what seemed then a terrible offence and it meant we were all assembled in the next room to hear the victim scream. Masters and mistresses had to listen too in their common room next door and when it was over a mistress asked the beaten one " was it on the bare ? " It was she who told us later when her young man died of wounds how he screamed when these were dressed. But then one remembers only the horrible of such times.

Our scoutmaster was a man with round hand-writing he was proud of. He never joined one letter to another, each was separate and formed as though he was not writing on flat paper but on small globes. He was fat and like all senior scoutmasters looked ridiculous in shorts and the comic opera hat. We used to go out and earn badges for lighting one fire with not more than three matches, and I remember how strange it felt to be trusted with anything so dangerous. Later, having got the badge for lighting fires we boiled potatoes in billy cans to get cooking badges.

I fell down and hurt my knee so they tied scarves across two scout poles in the way it is laid down in regulations and tried to carry me back. Each time they got me in, those scarves slipped dropping me through on to the road till they had to make me limp along with them. The one good turn a day was used on holidays at home as another excuse to fag one.

Another master drew illustrations all day long for magazines. He played football with us and would call out " use your wings," meaning of course the outside men but we used to flap our arms as though we could take off like swans. This seems to be one of the facts of childhood that you could make out to yourself you could fly if fired by some word and every other little boy there saw it as well and flapped his arms at once. They must be the perfect reading public for, if good writing is to evoke common, that is universal remembered feelings, then even if they are too young to have much to remember they do seem to have everything in common and are so quick to take it up.

This same man one day began something in his class which must be unique. He started handicapping. He found out where everyone stood by marks, numbered them, put me top to start from scratch, made each other boy plus something until the bottom one was plus six. He then marked us by merit in everything we did and added the handicap, or bonus marks for stupidity and lack of attention and counted these adjusted marks as his standard for the position of merit in his class. I could see it was aimed at myself and went on strike so that I fell to bottom of the form. At that time I thought it as unjust as anything could be but I think it brilliant now and a just foretaste, not so much of what I have found since for I have been lucky, but of what does go on around one.

In breaks when they went to their common room to smoke we went out on a playground next the swimming-pool and covered with sand in which we used to turn up round iron balls about an inch in diameter. What they were for I cannot think but they must have been there some time they were so corroded by the weather. We thought them lucky and in looking I for one went back to those days when I thought there was treasure in every corner or, more particularly, in that coal-hole Poole had known.

The swimming-pool, a paradise in summer, was old-fashioned and had no overflow.. They only changed the water once each week so that after six days' sun it was tepid dirty. With the water fresh it was spring cold and we screamed more than ever when the headmaster pushed us in. Women scream in swimming-baths and at the sea but they are not being like children then. As I see things it is sex in little boys makes them shrill out at times like these. They are so feminine they go on like women on the sands even when they can see no man within miles, scream after scream echoing up cliffs to the deserted top over which, and over a boy watching behind his tuft of grass a blade of which gets up his nose, sea-gulls soar on their white wings diagonally set to the sun-blue sky.

He made us put our hands above our heads and pushed us from behind. We fell smack upon our bellies, " dive in you little beast," and screamed from the shock of being cool and at the smile behind his dazzling sun-reflecting spectacles, under his moustache that glimpse of false teeth which showed us that he smiled.

For our hot baths, which like the lavatories were in two rows of cubicles and which we had once a week, the under-matron came in to each one of us to see we were getting clean. Later when my hair began to grow she came in no more but of course I did not connect the two. When I asked my master and he told me it was because my hair was growing I had no idea of what he meant and did not ask. That is probably why I remember it now, sex was a great mystery then, although not the great one yet, and questions unresolved stay in the mind.

I say my master because each smaller boy was " slave " to a bigger one. We called ourselves slaves and would carry his bats and pads out on to the field and so forth. I cannot tell whether our head-master knew of this system but you can be sure he did and that being so is proof there was nothing sinister in it. It had this advantage that if there was something you did not know you had this boy to ask, and mine told me if he knew. It started probably from the headmaster putting each new boy under the guidance of one older than himself from which it followed the new boy had to oblige his master, be a slave. It did not follow that his master had any further rights.

There was trouble later however. What it was I never found out though I can guess. The first day of term we were called in one by one to see him in his study, a room we hardly ever saw. He had started on the school list taking the top boy first and so on down and as he got nearer my own position so my apprehension grew. Those who had seen him would not say what it was about but they looked shaken and gradually we who had not yet been in came to realize this was not just another case of beating, they were not holding their bottoms or taking friends apart to show their wounds, this time it must be gigantic, it could not be less than expulsion. This so worked on me that by such time as I was called I was in a state I hardly knew what he was saying his face was so grim and it had been so long to wait. I came away from him stupefied with apprehension I did not know of what. He must have been vague with us younger ones for fear he might give us ideas. Whatever it may have been no one was sacked although as we soon found out one boy had not come back from the holidays. All that term he stayed grimmer than ever. Of course one sees now his living was at stake, at the mercy perhaps of one little liar.

There was less to be said for him in my last term when those who were leaving were all sent for to his room in order that, as we came to realize only some years later, he might tell us the facts of life. He began with butterflies, of course we knew about them, went on to bees and then to birds and then he thundered out: " D'you little nippers know the difference between men and women when they have no clothes." We were so thunderstruck we all said yes sir and I did too but I had no idea and I remember now he said, " well that's all right then " and seemed enormously relieved. He went on to say that after what he had said about butterflies and the rest we could work it out for ourselves if we remembered how different men and women were and ended with a warning against unspecified vice so appalling that I was as one who has heard too huge a noise, too vast a something that has not been disclosed; it was too much to take in and I was left, in no wise the worse for not knowing, in a void of unmentionables, or as they say all at sea.

So much at that time of what you did not know was threatening, Latin before one began to learn seemed it was going to be a trial, algebra before one came to it loomed in front. We were easily awed. When the railings of the drive were struck one day by lightning and we went out and smelled sulphur I for one thought it was God and so did several others. You could not be sure God would not strike and having no experience we did not know new things are much the same always, languages places countries, the next world if you like, but hardly ever people. At that time we thought the reverse, that all persons old enough to have left school had no difference of any kind and that being at school was strange as Tartary.

SCHOOL must seem strange at all times, it cannot be natural to go to school. It is no odder than the world outside, only more concentrated. So that when war was declared in 1914 our hysteria became a fair copy of what could be found outside the grounds only larger, we displayed it in purer form.

I can remember headlines saying WAR in bigger letters than any I had seen and nothing else at first, no one went to whom I had to say goodbye, my father was too old, my eldest brother not old enough yet. We slipped into war the creatures of a routine which did not vary and it was only gradually things began to be different.

Many boys had their fathers fighting and there was one such parent, a general who wrote every week to our old monster. When a letter came he had us all called together and then read what was in it. We followed how things were going with flag pins stuck into a large map put up over the scholarship board.

If we did wrong we were reminded they were out there fighting for us.

In the carpenter's shop each boy first made his own dummy rifle and was then turned on to making bed tables, the days of pipe racks and deck chairs were gone. My father has the pipe rack still I made in 1913 and there are still three bed tables at home the carpenter finished for me in the next three years which were used when our house became a hospital. Those I finished on my own have fallen to pieces as have the foundry patterns I made twelve years later in our factory. It is not a trade for amateurs.

Now we did no more gym but were drilled instead, no more boxing but dummy bayonet fighting. We formed fours twice a week, we shot with rook rifles on a miniature range. And was it then or some time later that, as our school was on the south coast, some formation of the hills round brought no louder than as seashells echo the blood pounding in ones ears noise of gunfire through our windows all the way from France so that we looked out and thought of death in the sound and this was sweeter to us than rollers tumbling on a beach.

As food began to get short we were put on to growing vegetables in the gardens. Twice a week we weeded and did jobs of the kind that were not too difficult. Being strong I was given a mallet to split firewood, another boy held the wedges. One day our old tyrant came and held these himself and I hit him smack on the thumb, splitting it open. He never said a word and walked away hiding his finger. He did not even hold it against me.

At one time in the year we went out to hoe turnips

on a farm near by, mangel-wurzels such as in happier days my mother had Poole roll across the lawn for her to shoot and we were so hungry we ate the small ones. The farmer, an enormous man, had been a weight lifter and to reward us when our work was done he gave a performance with those long dumb bells they use, made of iron painted black.

Food, always in our minds, began to haunt our dreams. Not that we were unhappy or obsessed only there was not enough and what there was of bad quality. I can remember hams more than high with gaps in the meat and a smelly clear liquid in these, plates and plates of rice and messes of lentils. But we never really had too little, no one's health was affected, it was only unpleasant and not something to go through again. Sunday stood out for that reason because on that day they gave us cake for tea extra to the slabs of bread with margarine we had on weekdays. And for lunch, as we sat all strange in our Eton suits, having been to Sunday service and finished our regulation Sunday letter home, there might be what was our favourite sweet of all, ginger pudding with treacle.

Sunday smelled, I do not know why, but that day perhaps because one had time to notice. It began with the school chapel which was heavily waxed to make the tortured wooden pews stand out, grained pine, and then the linoleum everywhere had been polished. Again, each Sunday afternoon we had a

walk still dressed in our best and we could draw
in the sweet country air, this island's attar of
roses, coming from the sea overland to where we
meandered, the woods all about us, rooks up in the
sky, the cattle in the fields. Every lane so it now seems
was sunken, tufts of grass and wild flowers overhung
our walks and sometimes, coming over the hill, we
had that view over all the county where it lay
beneath in light haze like a king's pleasure preserved
for idle hours; that was how we went within earshot
of the guns, chattering and happy through loveliness.

Almost in the town we were outside there was a
park they let us visit, a place of broad grass avenues,
the slopes on each side covered by trees and with
bracken which hid the deer. The great house it was
about hushed the whole place, was beautiful by
time, by its leisure and by something which even at
the age one was then was overwhelming. It was here,
on these Sundays, I began to have those first movements of delight, those first motions toward the open
heart which is growing up, taking one's place, looking
beauty right in her cow eyes.

There were other smells, and this is almost too
much one fears to be believed, as when there was an
epidemic of measles or another illness of that kind
and our headmaster had everyone wearing two pairs
of socks with garlic in between. This was indeed a
stench and our schoolmistresses went about like cats
found out, with haughty faces.

There was the smell of hot water when after football he made us take off our clothes and step into a trough sunk in the floor and here I first knew modesty, that shrink from mass nudity I still have, that shock, that feeling this is wrong which in my case is the strongest of all instinctive feelings. To this day I draw blinds and lock doors. I feel helpless with no clothes. I mind men seeing me naked more than women.

The war went on, more and more people were killed. When our mothers visited us they often had news of relatives who had lost their lives. When they came down they were allowed to take us out to tea in the town and it was a rule we had made between ourselves that each of these times we should take a friend with us. This rule was unbreakable and it so happened that when a friend's father lost his life and his mother came down to read out his last letters home I went out with them and after tea we sat in that park I have described and they both cried over his letters as we sat with our backs against a tree. You would have thought this rule could be relaxed at such a time but there was no question of it. We always had boiled eggs when out for tea.

Even so the war seemed remote and it was not until air raids started that I began to realize how close aeroplanes had brought it. This I believe was true of all of us, even of those who had lost near relations, for when some time later my eldest brother died it was not until his funeral that I really knew he was dead, and soon forgot afterwards. Out of sight is out of mind with little boys except their mothers.

Now our school was on top of a high hill and so placed that enemy aircraft tried to pick us up when they came over, or so we were told. In any case we were ringed round by anti-aircraft batteries. All at once when the batteries began firing we would wake to see over a dark horizon the vicious summer lightning of our guns and then the crack rattling the windows, more sinister far than thunder. They were some way off but even at the distance we were they were so searching and awesome, throwing up at each flash black outlines of trees between as they sought those planes out where they were flying in a veiled radiance between lighted cloud and moon soft sky above. We stole to the windows, taking care in all that abyss of noise to make no sound ourselves and watched, awed but not frightened until as often came about shrapnel began to fall spent on the roof. When this happened we did feel miserable and ran back to hide beneath the clothes.

Some time before this we had read of the Mons angels. You will remember they had been seen to come out in front of our line in France and by giving an illusion of great numbers had discouraged an enemy attack when this might have been disastrous. Our old tyrant, an Old Testament man, had been overwhelmed by this story and carried it to extravagance, it was proof to him, as it was to many others, that God was on our side. And as we followed him in everything he said we also utterly believed in this story. Now air raids, and not a boy had been hurt in one, attracted us because they were awe-inspiring without being dangerous. Also it made us proud to be under fire. In consequence we spent much time each night crouched by the windows waiting for another to begin. There we stayed until we got so cold and tired we went back to bed to be woken perhaps, only much later and only once and again, by the batteries firing. They were vigils.

Whether it was headlights of a car over our playing fields as they swung into the main road or whether it was, when there was a raid, the flash from the guns, whatever it may have been we were sure those same angels from Mons went across the upper playing fields our windows looked over. Almost every night we thought we had seen them. And as it was super-natural the oaths we swore to tell nothing of all this to the tyrant were kept. I do not think he ever knew.

It was typical of our society that when our elders believed these angels had been seen at Mons we believed we had seen them for ourselves. Even more typical we did not suppose they came to protect us, we were afraid of them, horribly afraid. And when it was put about that our old tyrant had admitted seeing them for himself, which I believe to be untrue, any doubts we may have had evaporated into the thin air our angels used for bone and skin.

Everyone began to behave so well in church that he asked, I remember hearing, some of the older boys what was on their minds but it had become a matter of conscience to tell nothing of all this. We believed, as we do now when we say do nothing to change your luck, that if once this guilty knowledge were given away the angels might have their revenge. Any secret, our old tyrant had warned us, must be guilty, the secrets we were not allowed to have for fear they might be sexual. Accordingly we kept quiet and in dread, learned without surprise that armies had marched through the Dead Sea and discussed trying to walk across our swimming-bath on top of the water. But as life became more mysterious it became more frightening and I think it is interesting that because they had been through air raids without one bomb being dropped within seventy miles boys should see what they took to be malignant ghosts of those who had died for them drifting across their playing fields.

Next morning we would go out and there was often shrapnel to be picked up. We used to put it with our parents' letters and the underclothes in that locker each boy had in his dormitory, our sacred hiding place. It had been safe for all our private things but now the maids began to steal this shrapnel where we had hidden the bits and we came to know

what we might have realized before that there was
no place of one's own in all the school, no getting
away.

Similarly when my uncle, commanding an Army
Corps in France, sent me some old maps of trenches
round Passchendaele, and how kind of him that was
to find time, our old tyrant took them away and
locked them up. He said he would give them back
when it was all over but he never did; being a child
is to have things taken from one all the time.

Any leisure we had we spent in knitting khaki
mufflers.

Another story preyed on us then, and, as I have
said before, one remembers only the horrible of
times like those. It was the tale of Germans being so
short of fats they boiled their own dead down with
ours to make food. This lie which we took for truth
gave me exactly those awed feelings I had when we
talked of sex. Sex was a dread mystery. No story
could be so dreadful, more full of agitated awe than
sex. We felt there might almost be some connection
between what the Germans were said to have done
and this mysterious urgency we did not feel and which
was worse than eating human fats; or so it seems
now, looking back on what many call their happiest
time.

Can it be true that people genuinely feel they were
happiest at school or is it because they are so miserable grown up? It may be they have not enough

routine to pass the time as they are now and that a time schedule, as for private soldiers in the army, is what they want, what they miss, and what in a war they will get.

Possibly they had more authority in those days without responsibility, is that why they say they were happiest then ? I only know I did not begin to live until I had escaped, except during the holidays. These were blissful and it is true there is nothing like them now.

WE had calendars and each boy marked off every day which brought him closer to term's end, as prisoners notch the walls. When that day came we had not slept all night and went off, piled up in vans, chattering like starlings when they come back. And then within a day it was home once more and their being glad to see me, even the servants, and weeks stretched out in front with everything one could want ready waiting until, but it was so far ahead one could forget, the time would come, the calendar day unmarked, when at last we should have to go back to school again.

Holidays spell summer days and they still mean evenings in August very hot, a mist in the elms about. Where we lived had once been forest land and in each hedgerow grew magnificent trees while down by the river, by the place they used to ford over, there was a giant's orchard of poplars. Higher up were oak trees, old as the forest, broken down and hollow although beautiful still, an order of old trees . which at one time had formed a glade. They were on a hill and standing on it to look across at Tewkesbury Abbey rising clear above the town from a huge

flat meadow which has always lain between, over
the weir which adds to the Severn's stream, looking
down right-handed between those riven oaks to
what was once the ford, it is a ferry now, I could see
where I was to start fishing, laying my rod in the
boat and rowing off upstream or down.

Part of everything there may be in fishing, in what
one remembers of it, is in coming over the hill to
that first sight of where one is to fish, where under the
withies nodding low into moving water chub lie in
wait to pick up what falls to them from those sharp
pointed leaves, or where, because I was no fly
fisherman yet, under an alder there was a hole I
knew where bream lay ground feeding.

When a wind came it was generally against the
stream which was fast enough to throw up waves as
the wind stroked it and fish did not take when there
were waves. So it was that I only went out on still
days, or rather late in the afternoon when the wind
had dropped.

Getting into my boat I could go left upstream and
begin fishing quite soon for there was only a short
pull to the weir or go right and, with the stream to
help, row half a mile to where there were long
stretches of bank dressed green in withies. If one
went up to the weir there might be others fishing,
mostly for eels it is true but one had to avoid their
punts and this was not easy drifting in a boat alone.
For my method was to drift just close enough to those

overhanging withies to drop my fly where they dropped into the water or into any hole in that descent of green wind or the weather might have made. So a fishing day had to be still or one would be blown too near, too far and if there were punts to keep clear of then it was too difficult. But nobody came lower down, for years I had it to myself, only it was farther so that there was always this choice to make, which way to go, up or down and in the end I always chose the same. If there was time and I had my lunch with me I went upstream and fished the weir first. If the wind did not drop until after tea then I would go downstream and fish into a glitter of the sinking sun breaking water into fields of blinding points of light like into diamonds set in coal in sunlight.

But a fly rod came later. At first there was float fishing at any spot handy to the house. Later of course one came to have a favourite place, that alder under which the bream lay unseen, flat as half-crowns or next to the first withybed in a run or swim where small chub would take or roach now and then. Once settled down the high bank and on a level with the water time stopped, one went on until it grew too dark.

Each small movement of the float was to be interpreted and there was anguish while it was moving in trying to decide when best to strike. One struck and missed to find the bait gone, and as I was most often

using paste I never knew whether the fish had taken
or whether I had torn off the bait in striking. One
never knew. Six hours could go by in a pleasing
suspense and it might be no fish had come near
where one was fishing.

After their day's work men would leave Tewkesbury in the evenings riding bikes along the bank
opposite until they came to where each always
fished. Setting up their rods they would settle down
across the river and to a boy there was something
conspiratorial in all of us hunched over our floats as
shadows began to stretch out long over the surface of
the water. Then or a little later the evening rise
began with a noise of smacking lips, ring after ring
was drawn and being drawn opened outwards in
larger circles. And last the bream began to jump
coming out of the water coloured like Victorian silver
coinage in that half-light when the fields are
shrouded, when night looms following a flood of
scarlet in the sky at evening.

It is said bream jump to clear the slime off their
scales but even if that is so it did not do to watch
them or the rise, lying in wait one had no time
to spare for now was the moment when the float was
not content to bob, it might be taken under in a flash
and be as suddenly released if one did not strike
instantly.

Another time the fish seemed to take was when
pleasure steamers paddled by, working up or down

from Gloucester. The wash their passage made stirred the fish and, just before the first wave got to where you were sitting and your float was sucked swooping towards it, was when you might have something so that even the lovers in each other's warmth on deck would look round as they were carried on to see what luck you had.

Again when there was a tide, for the Severn is a tidal river, it will rise perhaps as much as five foot in thirty minutes, this also seemed to put bream on the feed. It paid to alter the depth at which one was fishing every so often so as to fish no more than twelve inches off the bottom. For if the level rose the fish stayed where they had been even if one was retreating, cursing and anxious up the bank as the river crept up under pressure from the sea. All of us who were out had to do this and it was another bond between us, as was our fishing with those travelling on the river. Something which is best done alone is a companionable waste of time to watch. But it cannot be waste if nothing can take it away as nothing can, if before one goes to sleep at night one goes back to it under the blankets, one's thoughts like pigeons circling down out of the sky back to their dovecot set down where the river, sweeping to the sea, makes another turn like the last those birds make coming out of the evening.

And if there are things we seek to share, hunched now on the office stool, facing a slow death in the

shelter they have made our basement into, we might
as well turn back to when we stumbled home through
the dark, our faces still burning with the day's sun
and then tell ourselves as the syren goes and frightened we begin to forget, because we do not know if
we are going to be killed, how we did once find this
or the other before we go to die to take with us
like a bar of gold.

As I write now a war, or the threat of war, while
still threatening seems more remote; a change of
wind and the boat is blown in, there is nothing to do
but tie up and call it a day. That is the pity of
sobering down to middle age, there must be a threat
to one's skin to wake what is left of things remembered into things to die with. The crime is to forget.

So as one went downstream, casting to every likely
overhanging bush and sometimes coming to a withy
bed, that is to say a thicket of them in which they are
cultivated for basket making, so as one gained experience through fishing this stretch over and over
one came to know the likely places at which for some
reason not apparent above the water fish were in the
habit of feeding. In the Wye and on trout streams or
even higher up this same river with a dry year the
level of the water falls and the fisherman can see any
inequality in the river bed which, for the protection
it gives, attracts the fish as it lies head on to the
stream. But here the Severn never ran so low that
one could see the bed so that the knowledge one

acquired could only be obtained by trial and error which, being peculiar to oneself, was the more valued. There is no excitement apart from sex so keen as the approach to a favoured place in good conditions, no short suspense so pleasurable as dropping the fly just right and, not being able to see the fish, as waiting for the rise.

Too much has been made of playing a salmon or, with a fly, watching the trout come after it. There is a secrecy in wet fly fishing on the Severn with the fly out of sight and the skill lies in knowing more from the behaviour of the line than from anything on the surface of the water that a fish is taking it down. It is an exciting connection with a remote element when there is only a hint of what is going on so that to this day I would as soon go after trout and fish deep with a worm as use a dry fly.

But again this preference may come from having begun my fishing the way I did, the prejudice we all have for the things we did first, that " I don't know but I think I'd rather go after them over dogs the way we used to." Opinions of this kind are memories and memories of early days seem true. The earlier these memories may be the truer they seem and not only the earlier in time but rather anything one remembers of the start of an experience. One hears so many people say " when I first went into business a man came to me " or " when I was a boy my father said when they let you eat oysters see that they are good," and so on and equally fatuous but only told because it was the first time someone had tried to get by that way in business or because he could remember something about oysters going back to the days, but how remote, before he had ever tried them.

Thus when I first fished it was in the moat where there was nothing to catch except dead leaves. In my disappointment I changed over from the idea of catching fish to that of hauling treasure out which the monks who had built our house must have dropped for safety in the moat. It is not knowing what may be on the end of the line which is half the fun of sea fishing. Not being able to see but only to feel is what any fishing still means to me, particularly in the Severn because that is where I began.

My parents first sent me out with a man called Bassett. His peculiarity was that as he walked in those short trips he took from pub to pub on land he always leant his head back so that he could look up at the trees. Even when he rowed he watched the withies on the bank. He was looking for withybobs. These caterpillars feed mostly on withies but they can be found, always in colonies, on many other trees as well. He used them to bait the hook. He would string one on tail first putting the head in a noose of gut tied to the cast so that when you struck into a fish the bait would have shot up the cast as much as twenty inches. To fish again you just pulled it down to the hook. He it was who showed me where there was a run of gravel which you could reach only from a boat and which, as he died some time ago, I thought I was the only man left to know until the other day I was sorry to see two men in a punt from Birmingham fishing it and pulling them out.

He took me trolling for pike and every time he rowed past the pub by the ferry he made a remark about how dry his mouth had turned. But I had that shyness all children have of spending their pocket money, they are all misers small blame to them, so I turned him away. As when one day alone at the Zoo on Sunday, fourteen years of age, one of the lion's keepers thought me good for a tip and took me behind. When it was over and I had seen the cubs I told him I would recommend him to my father who was a Fellow. Another time a mason doing some work at the country house said " You be as mean as wood ashes."

MY parents kept horses and as soon as my two brothers and I grew long legged enough to get a grip of the saddle we were put up on ponies and taken out hunting by a groom on leading strings. There was a horse " Portlaw," an old favourite of my mother's but too old to carry her at that time, which the groom used to ride. This animal had been owned by a Master of Hounds and was never at ease until, as when moving off from the meet to draw, he was walking directly behind the hounds in that sacred gap between the pack and field. He would set his pace at a walk or trot which was rather faster than the others and would creep up on the field, passing through them until he had reached where we never should have been, where the bigwigs rode. It was the first embarrassment.

On hunting days we had poached eggs for tea when we got home, just as our parents did, and this was the first sign of growing up.

Later I outgrew my pony and wanted the larger one my brother rode. I could not have her because he had not outgrown her yet; in the same way I did not get his clothes until they were too small for him.

But I grew unreasonable and after one more season on my old pony no longer cared at all for hunting, all the more because when at last I got the one I coveted I found she kicked out going through gates. I had always known this, the red bow in her tail was there for all to see, but if one wants something enough one will ignore the disadvantages until they have been experienced. Never having been up on anything ill-behaved before I had no idea of how one could be classed with the animal ridden, that one could overhear others warning about how you lashed out in gateways, that " look out, here he comes again so we'd better get through first."

All I remember of those days is the excessive cordiality my elders used towards each other at the meet, the terror with which most of them waited while the covert was drawn, and the excessive rudeness which came over them in that first gallop there is after the hounds have found after which I would be left. Chipping, the groom, and I would make our way diagonally across the circles foxes usually make their way by; if you know where the coverts are and what they call the line foxes take then by diligently trotting, with time to spare to shut open gates, you can come up on the field quite often and then as likely as not be in danger of heading the hunted fox. My mother's father I believe went out with a servant who carried two axes in his saddle and because there was so much wire in his country (they were his own hounds) every variety of wire clipper as well and yet he saw as much as anyone of what went on. Those who, galloping hard and jumping everything, were seldom out of sight of hounds were seldom out of earshot of his voice encouraging his man as he chopped the fences down, for my grandfather had lost his nerve and would not jump. After hunting so they say he would go out in his pink coat, still in his boots and play golf in the park with his butler in a bowler hat carrying the clubs. Those in fact were other days even more remote than 1912 though 1912 seems strange enough when what they are going to use to kill us was not even invented, just a toy or a dream fidgeting the inventor.

Those were the days when everyone rode home, there was no riding then to the nearest telephone and waiting for the car to pick you up. Riding home after a hard day has been sufficiently described, every fox-hunter brings it in to one of his books. It is like coming after football to a hot bath, it has been hard exercise in the open and you feel what you so often hear described " that delicious feeling of tiredness." Feelings of that kind depend on peace of mind, they are luxuries for those used to luxury. No more than hard exercise will give a sense of work well done. As such it is more than enough to entrance little boys, to make them feel important and all the more as Chipping would often let me ride Portlaw home, so high off the ground after my pony I felt I was balanced on an awkward steeple.

As they got near the drive and knew they were home the horses would prick their ears and this would give one that sense of something shared, which, ironically enough, when it happens to be with animals is better remembered than one of those we have so readily in talk, known by so many phrases such as " a click " or " then we got together."

Hunting is enjoyable also because many a run entails a variety of misfortunes for those trying to keep up, misfortunes which, unless badly left behind or out of sight which it is hard to be—there is a witness behind every hedge—can be retailed and are sure to arouse interest if one's family is keen and has been out. Someone has lost a stirrup or staked his horse or has taken the most awful fall and for children this is the first exchange they have on the level of and with their parents, discussion of ideas having only too naturally no appeal to either side. " They ran hard right up to Volter's and that was where I first saw him being carried on a gate."

But hunting was spoiled for me because I was a coward, my not having the pony when I wanted it being that kind of excuse one uses to explain oneself away and I liked shooting no better. We used to go out walking partridges and my father always put me on the outside of the line. Through marvellous September weather year after year we went after them and each September they grew less as more land was put down to grass. Some years they were so few we would pursue two coveys all day until exhausted on a hill we lay down while the two keepers thought they could see one or the other covey running, a platoon in broken order down below, where we could hear them faintly calling.

We had no snipe at all though there were floods enough and we often went out after them. It was a delusion and is one still with the keepers, it still recurs, that they have seen or heard them on their rounds.

But all this in the most beautiful country. Of course one was lucky to have these chances and lucky to find out early on this was not the life to pine for. It is expensive taking long weekends as many do to inaccessible spots in Wales and distressing to come back to London Sunday evenings with one's heart still beating by a marsh near Builth perhaps. In the end it kills those who have to work in town. It breaks their hearts not to get over the longing.

Pheasant shooting was more fun, or at least I liked it better because I enjoyed beating, getting into thick places and yet trying to keep in line. When allowed to carry a gun it was no hard work at all, one's place was marked out by a stick cleft at one end and in that cleft a piece of folded paper like a message from the gods, and all one had to do was stand and shoot. The keepers whistling their dogs, the strange chuckling noises the beaters made—a cruel parody of panicked hens, the burst of wings when a pheasant got up which is so sudden if one is walking through a wood alone, the maniac laughter—cruelty again—with which the beaters keep a rabbit up, the cry " hold hard on the left," and then the tap tap of sticks until the right hand end of our line has time to beat the brambles out: all this perhaps under threatening skies with a drop on every twig from rain which had stopped coming down and here again, waiting at the end, tea and the blazing fire and that unreasonable sense of something accomplished so that, as we sat around, our voices rose, oh self assertion!

Part of the pleasure lay in how much the dogs had enjoyed the day. After they had been dried in the pantry they would put themselves close by the chairs where, still shouting about ourselves, our hands reached down to free their ears of burrs while they looked into the fire, into its heart.

But all of this came to an end although it is still today the same, the first few times were soon over and then it was the war.

All through my life I have been plagued by enjoying first experiences too much, and that is true also of my first experiences of new people. How wonderful they seem the first few times, how clever, how beautiful, how right; how nice one seems to them because so interested, how well it all goes and then how dull it becomes and flat. I spend my time thinking there is nothing to say and people are always saying to me, " what is the matter ? " It is a question of animal spirits and this is true also of field sports and that is why we look to the bottle when in company, drink being the best refreshment for all the senses. But during the war it was fresh faces every holidays.

It was a large house and in 1917 was turned into an officers' convalescent home, taking in about twenty at a time. As these officers were badly needed back in France they did not stay for long. Each holiday from school there was a new outfit and better still we got the most marvellous food because we were feeding them up to go back to be killed.

Desperately bored, terrified of going back to France, many with no idea of country life and most of them trying uncomfortably to seem at home in a country house they found in me a boy who looked on them as heroes every one and who enjoyed each story of blood and cruelty they had to tell. One in particular I shall not forget of the middle aged German who each morning went to do his duty behind a stump instead of going to the latrines. The stump was some distance off and modesty made him put it between him and his own lines. He was out of rifle range but the artillery officer could see him through glasses and the problem was how to get the range to blow him up without frightening him away. They

spent days in working it all out and with the first
shell they sent over they got him.

Then there were the airmen with fantastic tales,
one man had fallen without a parachute three
thousand feet smack into a haystack, but in the end
my parents had to say they would take no more of
them, they were all so nearly dead, it was suicide to
serve in the Air Force, that they could not what we
called behave themselves. They had been so close to
death they had a different view of life and this made
them what we called difficult, or, after yet another
escapade, impossible even. They were people meant
to die, they did not fit into life and in no respect into
life as we knew it.

As we knew it was in a big house where the family
had been for one hundred years. There is a Great
Hall, a large room and high as the house with black
oak beams set back into the V-shaped ceiling, a
library with numbers of books given as prizes,
sitting-rooms, passages hung with prints, wood fires
and great comforts with good beds. Into this which
had been built up with care and a kind of neutral,
anxious taste by great-grandmothers grandmothers
and mothers each altering in her turn, into this
Morris pot, for so it was decorated then, stylishly
decorated to receive those known to its owners like a
few bumble bees in an old hive, the house dated from
1392, into the home and this house for the weekend
relative who was visiting about was poured this

curious life of men who for a while were safe but who killed and were killed, being paid for it. Before they came however there was the Australian soldier.

My brother had died while still at school and my mother felt she could no longer go on nursing at the hospital she was in, she could not sleep and found the work too hard. So she took this man who had been gassed during the first gas attack and then while he had lain under a wet sack fighting to breathe had been blown up by a shell only to be buried at once by another. He was no longer human when he came to us. He committed suicide when he left to go home, he found the bustle on board ship too much for him.

Unattractive in every way, small, ugly, with no interests one could find, he had haunted eyes as though death to which he was still so close and which walked arm in arm with him through our meadows could be a horror worse than what he was still suffering. He did not sleep, he hardly ate, he shook all day and he was like an old specimen jar which is cracked and irreplaceable, others are made which may be better but they do not know how to make them the same, so cracked that a shout will set up vibrations enough to shatter it in jagged pieces, so that if one laughed he always screamed. If forty yards away you banged the door he screamed.

Towards the end he thought and we thought he was getting better and he told me he would like to go for a bicycle ride.

I asked him how he felt and he said he was all right. I asked him how far he would like to go and he said he could get to Chaceley church, three quarters of a mile away. I did not ask if I could take him, he was so old and I was ten, but I did ask him again when we had gone four hundred yards how he was feeling and he said he would manage nicely. We got to where the road goes round the church and then we came back. He was soon wobbling but he would not get off to rest until when we got into the drive he could just get off his bike and zig zag into the house not wishing I suppose that I should see him fall. He was up again in four days and it did not do him any harm but it damaged me and somehow, because he was ill he was acute, although he never spoke of it again I think he knew because it was not until then I realized by sharing it with him, how hopelessly far gone he was. We grow up by sharing situations, what we share of another person's increases us, and my memorial to all of them at that time in my heart now is my anguish remembered as I saw him stagger in disclosed, wondering whether perhaps it were not my fault.

The wounded officers had not only been so close to death they were made different by it, they were apart from us, I came to learn, by another close shave, birth. Some of them were made to go so far they even married the servants we had at the time. I had no idea this was possible. I knew nothing about fornication, but I did know you did not marry servants. When my mother sent me out of the room as she had begun to do when she had to talk over one of our officers with my father at week-ends, I felt sure it had to do with proposals of marriage. In fact of course it had to do with how they could be made to propose.

In the war people in our walk of life entertained all sorts and conditions of men with a view to self-preservation, to keep the privileges we set such store by, and which are illusory, after those to whom we were kind had won the war for us. That is not to say the privileged did not fight, we did, but there were too few of us to win. The effect of this on a child of my class was to open before his feet those narrow, deep and echoing gulfs which must be bridged, narrow because after all they were officers, deep because in most cases they had as civilians to come over that rope bridge over that gorge across which intercourse is had on the one side by saying " sir " and on the other " my good man." That is to say I began to learn the half-tones of class, or, if not to learn because I was too young, to see enough to recognize the echoes later when I came to hear them. Manners I know now were what they had not got. Before they had been promoted and before they had joined up as privates they had not had the money or the time to cultivate an attitude to others different in circumstances from their own. Manners may be a way of making, say, kings and peasants easy together under a roof, they may come from a confidence in himself which is the usual attribute of the moneyed person. We had those manners and I believe my parents made everyone easy at our hospital, but what was interesting was the effect on them and on myself.

One of the first took out my father's gun, his cartridges and his dog and shot his pheasants out of season without asking. I remember what upset us as much was the behaviour of my father's dog, that it should lend itself to such practices.

Others played poker for more than they could afford.

I forget all they did, but what had to be arranged was that the senior officer had to be given some control; maximum stakes were fixed and it was his part to prevent whatever abuse of hospitality they contemplated. In this way manners were ruled by discipline and so they became something else, bad manners became an offence against authority and in this way at once came near to what I knew at my private school.

When little boys go to school they begin to live two lives with two sets of values, as we do now in business and when in the evening we go home. I had been taught to be polite at home because all boys must behave; at school because if I were not then I should suffer for it. And so there were no

65

manners at school because there was no time for them and because it was easy not to be caught and conversely I was very polite at home where there was all the time in the world.

To extend this argument on manners, and by that I mean behaviour generally and how it is expressed, the best manners I ever met were those used by the villagers. In this case they were less a deceit than they can be, and came from the villagers having time and also from the relationship between us being a fixed one with simple rules. In talking with them the minutes would slip by with nothing vital said, in ease and comfort, with no flattery but with a high sense on both sides of things untold. In nearly every case the subject would be health, the politest of all forms of conversation.

Every Christmas my parents made a present to each mother of either, I think, a pound of beef or several yards of flannel, and it was my part to call on those my mother could not reach to ask which they preferred. This practice had been carried on by my grandmother and by my great-grandmother, so that the dilemma presented no surprise and each wife I saw had made her choice some time. And yet they were so polite, it took so long before one could mention why one had come and then when the choice was put it was received with such exquisite surprise that it was an education when at last after oriental wavering one was told a pound of beef, an education in how things should be done between people differently placed by the accident of birth and cash.

Again, on another occasion on this round to find what each cottager had chosen for her present, I knocked at one house where, for some rare cause—a disgrace I believe, not one of us had knocked in years. I had been told not to call there and had mistaken the cottage. I was brilliantly received and when the preliminaries were done at last and I put the question, was told I had made a mistake plainly but in such a way I left feeling the lady had not condescended but had put me in my place, back where at the moment through no fault of hers my family belonged, that is, not on terms with her own.

In peace time we have a life to live and in war of course hardly more than our lives to lose, and in this perhaps our hospital, it was really a convalescent home, was influenced, as I have shewn, by the imminence of death. But there was more than that. As we let those officers in, not one of them with an idea of country life as we knew it, so we let in life as it was to be after the war was over together with its slang and put into their heads an idea of how it must have been before the war came in this way of living, of its owners not directly earning the full income their mode of life incurred. That is if manners come out of money or time for reflection then after the war there was less of both. As I was too young to have realized how things had been I could not appreciate this but what I did learn for the first time is that there was a life not unlike that at my first school. Life at school had up till then been so remote from what I knew at home that I had thought it was more an interlude than what I came to know it as, a start. If growing up is to have a shrewd idea of what is coming then I began to grow up in this atmosphere of clerks aping gentlemen with swords, purblind auctioneers who could still fire heavy guns, and all the stink and boisterousness of war and the middle classes.

But they were heroes to me and were so kind they would always play. There was as well the delicious food we had because of them, clotted cream and any amount of butter, things which in those days were so impossibly remote as to seem barbaric delicacies of which one had read and yet would have no chance of tasting. I played for hours with them, it was as though I were in a university, privileged in spite of my age and listened all the time to those endless stories about Poperinghe, the Marne, the Somme.

We hated Germans and at school we did believe they were so short of food they boiled the dead down to get the fats, that they crucified Australians, and that they were monsters different from us. It is interesting to see how these atrocity stories are coming back today; as I write there are tales of concentration camps as bad as any told when Belgium was invaded in 1914. Again a month or two ago in September 1938 there was that authentic note of wild hysteria to recapture which you need only look at any war-time *Punch.*

Hysteria we had in that hospital, not such as haunted the poor Australian or the kind, woman fed, which was kept up behind the lines by those who did not do the fighting. We had screams in the night when they had dreams and I do not mean that but rather the sort which is veiled by jokes as when they were to come up before the Medical Board to have decided for them if they were well enough to go back to fight again.

Once when I was older and we were sitting at peace on the lawn one Sunday evening, my father said " I can't bear to think of going back to the office tomorrow morning, it is like going back to school." I agreed to be polite but I remember thinking there could be nothing so bad as when one's holidays from school were over and also promising myself I would never forget this, never think the same when I was his age and I had laid the books on algebra for ever down. I had forgotten the men told by these three doctors when they were fit to go back again to die.

We had about one hundred men who passed through the hospital and of those there was only one who wanted to go back to France. He was very young and had been wounded in the neck within three hours of his first getting to the front. He was always being chaffed about his neck, it made him carry his head at an angle; but as the time of the Medical Board grew near and he said at lunch he would beg them to send him back it was as though he had gone too far, as he had indeed, and said something indecent before the ladies. He was shunned after that.

It was hysteria too perhaps made people quarrel for no good reason at that time. Two respected aunts of mine argued at lunch one day whether the British soldier attacked with as much gusto as the French. I had not yet seen grown up relations quarrelling. They began quietly and became more quiet, using an exaggerated courtesy which first made me suspect what was to come and then, all too soon, began to quote what their husbands or relations who were serving out in France had told them. The trouble came because the one had higher authorities than the other which forced this one to hint that her brother, who was only a captain, had better cause to know than my other aunt's husband who was on the staff. At this my mother spoke and said, " My dears, not in front of Henry," but they were off and for the first time I came to know that in rows, when both sides have lost their tempers, one was wrong as a child to think one's elders had forgotten the schoolroom or rather that, when they lost their reason through being violently irritated, they came out no better than children who kick each other under the table. My mother and I went out, we left them to it, and I remember the sense of grown up complicity it gave me to go off with her because they were being so foolish.

But if then one grew up in the forced atmosphere of war under a strain which went on but which did not directly stress one, and as with the opportunities this strain gave to every child to see the cracks in the façade people put up before children in my circumstances, sleeping as I did at home alone and so with less chances to see people at bay, I came to know there was no great difference between ages and to guess that twenty years can go by fast. They can go by so quick the only difference is that at the end one may be far more tired, thinking much the same about everything only blunted. So I believe that my opinions then about people, who were at that time the extent of my experience, were the same as I have now but probably sharper, only always with two points of difference.

There were two urges made more urgent by the hysteria of the times and these of course were drink and sex. They are two hopeless barriers for children. If children try all they can, as I did, never to tell anything about themselves to their parents, and if they have this feeling it is hereditary and they cannot help themselves, then they are encouraged in it by these two things their parents probably never discuss before them. Even if parents take trouble to discuss sex in front of their sons the barrier of their being too young to participate would in my case have still helped me to keep all I could to myself in that instinct for privacy boys have who dream.

What I remember being so terrifying about these two things is that in both I had an idea they were shady actions. That is to say people went away somewhere to do them, whatever was done was not in the light of day, and they made people different. Accordingly, while I lived in this convalescent home in the sort of favoured position a mascot may be in, I was aware of these things I did not know which turned out to be sex and drink and which in fact, as it was war time, were the urge to life down there where we made men well to die and where each quarter of the hour was struck by the Abbey clock sweet and clear over our river and cattle in the meadows.

Years later, working through my father's factory in Birmingham, I had exactly the same impression when in the lunch hour I listened to some men unenviously discussing the lives of the rich. They took the usual ribald line taken in company about something one would like to have and has no chance to get and then, as so often in such conversations, they turned to how such riches could be acquired. There was so great a difference in the money (though, as I was in a position to know, comparatively so little difference in their lives) that sitting on a box part in the black sand I saw thousands struggling to get that life I had been born into and saw it as those men did who were too wise to bother much, and through their eyes as a promised but forbidden country rather idiotically strange. I remembered how when I was small I had had almost the same idea of sex only I had thought it terrible although I thought kissing idiotic. And the terrible was appalling in those days, one has only to remember dreams when one's digestion loosed tigers in the dark.

Our officers swam the river at night blind drunk and were all but drowned, the lane which went to Tewkesbury on the other side has ever since been known as lovers' lane, one of them, delirious from pneumonia saw babies on his bed in such numbers my mother was not surprised to learn he had four wives living and had never been divorced. All this and more went on around that I was not to learn till later, I only caught the echoes of it all and ominous they seemed.

Another had tried to commit suicide in his bath by cutting his wrists, so that, taken with my brother's death which had occurred a year before while he was still at school and with the lists of the dead each day in every paper, there was an atmosphere of death, and of the dying.

THIS feeling my generation had in the war, of death all about us, may well be exaggerated in my recollection by the feeling I have now I shall be killed in the next. Also anyone who was young at that time, too young to fight that is, would naturally if he has imagination make much out of what he remembers as he goes over and over it afterwards as we all do. But when my brother Philip died it brought death close enough.

I had not seen much either of him or of my other brother Gerald. When they had a governess I was still in the nursery and when in time I went for walks with my governess and they were back for their holidays from school they would be out shooting. The difference in our ages made a wider gulf between us than exists between officers and cadets, or apprentices and artisans; in that way seniority at school, which persisted into the holidays, is more like that graded life which we are told is spread through the associations built throughout authoritarian states to control the leisure moments of their peoples. I hero-worshipped both my brothers in much the same way I later came to worship our officers, it is true they had no uniforms and had not fought in battle but they were older, although younger than my parents and thus at home were like group leaders coming next to high authority, as the officers came next to generals and so forth.

They were already much too good at games to play cricket or football with me but Philip did take me out to that yard paved with brick and throw cricket balls to make me not afraid to play forward to the rising ball. He was very good at work and games. Now and again he would let me come and watch him smoke a pipe when he was still not allowed to do this. He smoked it under a hedge so placed that we could not be seen from behind and in front of us all of a long field so he could put it away before anyone coming could see what he had had in his mouth. A silly sight we made no doubt, a boy of nine adoringly watching one of fifteen smoke, but that is all, almost all I can remember of him. I was too young to be fond, all I could do then was to admire and then it was too late.

The first I knew of Philip's illness was when our old tyrant, going his round of the dormitories, sat down on my bed, a recognized mark of favour, and said he had been up to see him in London that afternoon. He told me Philip had been ill with great cheerfulness as if he were better, but that night I dreamed he was dead or rather that we had both of us died and were being received for some kind of

judgment into a presence. Some days later I was
called into the old devil's study to be told my
brother was dead. It meant absolutely nothing to
me at all. He took off his spectacles and became
helpless because he minded Philip dying, and I
remember being frightened I was not showing
enough sorrow. I had not learned by then to ask
for those details which in almost every case, and
certainly in his, are such as to raise a feeling of pity
which in turn will become self-pity; it was the first
death, and when the old man told me to sit on in
his room alone I cried because I thought I had to
cry, because there had been a disaster and because
here I was sitting unfeeling in this school holy of
holies, all alone.

I went up to London but the funeral was in the
country and I cannot remember going down there
or whether it was summer or winter. Everyone was
strange and I had a horror of the room where he lay
dead as though something alive were in it. I did not
go in but used to lie awake wondering how his face
looked though in the day I chattered to try to
distract my parents.

It was not until the country funeral and the sight
of so many I knew dressed in strange clothes and
their faces dressed in that special look people wear
on those occasions so strange to me then, that looking
you straight in the eye as you come down the aisle
without smiling, that showy gravity people never

have unless they are acting—all this and the coffin on old friends' shoulders, that is the estate servants, themselves in unfamiliar clothes but with something shared on their faces, the procession, the grave, the lowering of it in and then those dreadful words, the best the Church can do, the Church which seeks to share in all those few moments when we stand alone, at birth, in marriage, and at death, all this by its strangeness made me realize as we walked back along the path we always used on Sundays and brought it in to me at last.

Then I did cry on the way back, in self-pity of course at the menace.

When I went back to school the old tyrant was very kind to me. As he had been disappointed of a possible scholarship to be won when he found some months before I was not up to scholarship standard, and had showed it, this new attitude of his made a great difference. For death, in our school at least, put a plate-glass window between those whose family had been visited and the other boys; we shunned anyone thus afflicted, and when it happened to us were shunned in our turn. The reason was, I remember perfectly, that any boy was made strange to us, he was set apart by the occurrence as though he had turned overnight into an albino. This in individual cases did not last for long but during the war the grounds usually had one forlorn minute figure walking alone not feeling anything most likely but left to himself because he ought to be. Oddest of all was the effect this convention had when one of us died at school. I believe he put his finger down his throat and had the bad luck to scratch it, at any rate and despite the prayers the tyrant led us in both night and morning, he died quite soon and then we all of us walked alone for ten days out of deference to what we thought would be expected and also undoubtedly from a sense of shock.

After the funeral I had a great sense of shock whenever Philip's name was mentioned, and for some months had difficulty in not crying when someone said it out with no warning. So, much later, when in love and I heard the person's name unexpectedly, —is there anyone who has not felt their heart lurch then and, if it happens to be secret, combined with that same sense of guilt I had over Philip's death. For our old devil could not help evoking Philip when talking to me and always to my disadvantage. He did not do this cruelly or with any wish to hurt, he was just an old man with two sons at the war who was devoted, whenever he remembered them, to almost every boy who had left his school. When they were killed, and this was always happening, he minded dreadfully each time. He minded about Philip and it was natural for him to say " Henry, Philip would never have done that."

It was as natural for him as it was for the man who cut my hair in Tewkesbury who had a wooden leg to say as he did one morning not long after it happened, " I hear you lost your brother." I stammered something and I suppose he must have seen my face in the glass for he did not go on but I remember resenting his having as I thought been so indelicate. It seemed at the time more than anything the headmaster had ever put over on me. In fact it was a sign of the old man's ascendancy that we resented nothing he did, he was past criticism.

About that time also began the habit preachers grew into when they came down to school chapels, a habit which lasted well into what we called the Peace, of reminding boys every Sunday of the fathers, brothers and uncles who had died for them. At first we paid attention but in the end we had had so much there was no room for more. Similarly when I was giggling in class as one did then, uncontrollably and with that wild delight which turns into a natural phenomenon like sunlight so that one can't stop any more than one can keep the sky from shining on a field, then when I had to stop or be found out and punished I used to think of Philip. At first this always worked, then it sometimes did until at last I had to fall back again on biting my lips inside the cheeks until they bled. And that is so obviously the saddest thing about good friends who die, that one forgets.

In the beginning, however, it was bad enough, worse even than it was at home through the first

holidays. He could not stop recalling Philip and each
time the others would look round, their eyes blank
with that ostracism which, as has been described,
death at our academy brought with it. But with time,
and this was my horrible forgetting, I came to welcome his references, for no doubt these were growing
fewer as he began to forget. At last I began, if not
actually to long for them on a day when he did not
mention Philip, then at any rate to accept, when he
slipped one in again, with a smugness which passed
for piety.

This smugness persisted as we shall see later but
it will serve now to explain a discreditable scene
played it must be at about this time. There was a
boy, sufficiently unpopular, whose last term it was,
and whose friend I was supposed to be. When the
man with a barrow of sweets called on the last week
of term it was a custom, which was invariable and
sacred, that those who were leaving should spend
more than the sixpence doled out to them each week
and buy a sweet however small for everyone in the
school. Having bought them he had to go round,
seek each person out, and force a sweet on him
however much, in deference to custom, any one
might protest he had had enough. My friend bought
sweets but offered none to a soul.

It must have been absurd to watch the school
prowling round, not asking but very much expecting
the offer which never came. At last they revolted.

They all set on him and it was while he was running away before they caught up that I felt it was my duty to suffer with him because I was his friend. What helped to bring me to this pass was that he ran by me into the gymnasium with forty of them howling after and I, who had been so full up to that time of the story of Judas, I believe it haunts all little boys, went in after them to stand up for my friend.

He was at bay not with his back against a wall but in the middle of the gym between the rings we swung on, the ropes we had to climb, the parallel bars and the leather horse put back against the side. The floor was of yellow waxed parquet blocks, the walls red brick and the V-shaped roof in brilliantly varnished pine, a more violent yellow than the floor. We were all of us dressed in breeches made tight at the knee and in Norfolk jackets, most of us wore our brothers' suits, with long and violently untidy hair because it was soon to be one of the hairdresser's visits, a day or two before we were to go home. One or two smaller boys were sitting on their wooden lemon-coloured boxes set against the wall and some more sat with temperatures on the gold radiators, a thing those with temperatures always did when it did not pay to be ill, because they might be kept back and, so we thought, perhaps not go home at all. They did not join in, they were the audience there always is at school.

They were screaming at him, hating in him everything they hated, exulting in the revenge they

81

were going to have through him on the whole term, on everything which had gone wrong for each one of them. Reading this you may think they were going to do something terrible but this is not the case; all they wanted was to carry out the traditional mass punishment and that was, believe it or not, to all of them pile themselves up and lie on top of him.

I forget how I got in but at last they leaped, we lay down, and they piled up on us with groans and shrieks of rage at first and then of pain. I found what I had suspected, that those at the bottom get hurt least, and so it ended except that I was so proud; I thought it so brave and, I remember well, so Christ-like.

But it must not be thought that there was persecution or even prolonged unhappiness at our school. No one remembers happiness easily unless it is connected with some person or a particular event. In my case there were no persons except the headmaster and no events, our days were so arranged that there was always something happening to keep us out of trouble; nothing happened that was not arranged. We had no time to ourselves and so at that age were extraordinarily gay. We laughed, we screamed and shouted and went about in packs, every now and then we had a match against another school and tried tremendously to win but all this, apart from a general feeling I have that I was very happy there, all this has gone and what is left are the blows, the few things in such a pleasant time that hit one.

ANYONE who writes what he remembers of his own time is in a difficulty with names, he has to decide whether he will mention the living, if he is to call them by their real names when he does mention them and, if he chooses to alter the names they are known by whether he will disguise the place it all happened to him, and so perhaps find himself writing fiction.

This difficulty is increased when the name, if it is to be put down, is well known because the reader will have his own opinion of the place or person and it will be hard to convince him if one's own view is not his. Again the writer has to live, he has to go on meeting people many of whom no doubt have no desire to be recognized by comparative strangers in a book written by someone they dislike.

Another way is to mention only those who have died but my trouble here is that not enough have died yet.

The best way, and that which comes nearest to my style of living, is not to mention names at all. When I think of someone I see their face or something about them, it may be their hands, and often have difficulty in putting names to faces. Names distract, nicknames are too easy and if leaving both out as it often does makes a book look blind then that to my mind is no disadvantage. Prose is not to be read aloud but to oneself alone at night, and it is not quick as poetry but rather a gathering web of insinuations which go further than names however shared can ever go. Prose should be a long intimacy between strangers with no direct appeal to what both may have known. It should slowly appeal to feelings unexpressed, it should in the end draw tears out of the stone, and feelings are not bounded by the associations common to place names or to persons with whom the reader is unexpectedly familiar.

The public school I went to was down by a river in a deadly stretch, the main buildings were medieval and depressing, only the chapel was beautiful. Round and about these main buildings were the houses in which the boys lived, at this school one to each room. Where I came from firs had been planted by those new brick walls covered with raw copper-coloured creepers, here now in early autumn elm trees spread out their leaves and roses grew up the older brick of our houses. A magnolia had grown along between windows. My room, believe it or not, looked over the graveyard on one side of the chapel, which was a great high church without a tower and with rocketing flying buttresses. Under the moon I was frightened at first to look on to it so old in grey flaking stone the moonlight made black and half white so still over the graves, the windows seeming to listen for one's breath on those September evenings.

Almost always the chapel was deadly quiet but on winter nights towards Christmas they might have a carol service when the lights inside shone no brighter than a warmth through those gigantic pointed thumb shaped windows. The voices, as the song rose, came out to me with such confidence in my warm bed befuddled with sleep that they made a comfort of the day that was done. They became a part of everything, of one's life and of one's mossed death of sleeping. These days belonged to adolescence, when one's heart was the world's and at times one had then and only then universality of feeling. That is the nostalgia we have for school, or for summer holidays at home, because we felt we shared the world. We were fresh and saw opening out before as a promise what stretches at our feet now forever unredeemed.

One took more pleasure in food. Who is there who does not remember the salad bowls filled with bananas sugar and cream which the shops put out. Later on there would be crushed strawberries sugar and cream in bowls as big but neither of these until the war was over which happened in my first term and chocolate became chocolate again. That summer the parents took my brother and I to

Holland, a trip given over to eating. It is impossible
to forget the butter. Drab as we had lived all through
the war with margarine this heavy luxuriance went
to our heads and we ate so much there, we cut so
deep into solid golden yellow cow fed on Dutch
buttercups that after three days we were all of us ill,
and of course bad tempered. They had sweets there,
they have still, a sort of coffee toffee. We ate much
too many of these and indeed too much of everything
because we had begun to forget these things existed.
But at my public school when I was in funds and
when, as soon came about, there was plenty of
everything for sale, eating was a joy one would have
to train for now with plenty of exercise incompatible
with office work. It was sugar one wanted then all
day and which gave such joy to eat. Now it seems
I cover everything with salt, a sort of dry craving
which cannot give the pleasure sugar did. And so it
is too late for fruit salads, it is probably alas too late
to have that appetite ever again which made eating
so wonderful one ate so fast there had to be pauses
to draw breath and wipe the chin.

At The Hague, in the first hotel I had ever slept the
night, I took a bath and did not lock the door
because the room was private to the suite we had
taken. As I sat my mother's maid came through the
door and when I exclaimed went back again
apologizing. She had not seen more than my head
but I was so shy I thought I had insulted her. I

imagined she might think I had purposely not locked myself in. The next three days I apologized whenever I saw her alone, so much so and with such innocence, that she might well have suspected I had designs. It was my first embarrassment with a girl and later in that same week there was another, far more acute and almost inexplicable. We had gone to stay with a Dutch cousin at his country house and there was something I wanted, hot water or a collar stud. Fully dressed I opened the door and saw a housemaid working in the passage, fat and pink. I asked for whatever it was in English. She had no English and burst into giggles and I giggled too. As one sees it now she meant me to kiss her which I never did and of course this kiss which was not exchanged has lasted on where others given or received would have escaped the memory. Indeed it has grown, for better or for worse this incident now at this moment looms quite large and that I believe because of its impact; one was new then.

At that age one had an appetite for food, an appetite just beginning for girls, and for games though this last in my case was not to stay for long. Our school was arranged by houses each of which took between forty and sixty boys. Every house had a team and there was another for younger boys who were under sixteen. Some weeks were spent in settling these two teams and then came a knockout championship between the different houses.

87

Partly because our school was so old and partly from snobbery we played a medieval football in no way like any modern game except that we used a ball and goalposts. It was a miserable substitute for Soccer. It is true that we could not handle the ball but the tactics were to dribble it all bunched up together. The backs often practised long kicking, it was thought correct to volley the ball, and we had to follow up in a crowd. If they kicked too far the opposing back could volley the ball in his turn for his side to follow up and we had then to rush back to avoid being put offside. Accordingly one tore up and down ineffectively enough but at first I enjoyed it no doubt because everything was strange and the safest way to avoid trouble if one may not be going to fit is to take as great a part as possible in what is going on. At school one cannot keep quiet and be ignored, the boy who does not take his part is marked out, an albino through some fault of his own no matter what, and he must, the others feel, at all costs be dragged back to the fold if only to be made the butt of all.

Whether I enjoyed playing then because it kept me on terms or whether it was that I just enjoyed it I do not know but to be a part of the crowd was reason enough owing to the peculiar social structure of the place, the same as at all public schools.

There was a chairman, a vice-chairman, a managing director who was the headmaster, and a board

of directors, or, put in another way, a president,
who was a Leader, that is to say a man who has done
so well by his country that in his old age they make
him President, his deputy, then a go getter who did
all the work (the headmaster) and lastly the Cabinet.
This is an authoritarian state so run that the Prime
Minister could chop off heads without reference even
to his Cabinet. Under the Headmaster came the
housemasters or if you like the District Leaders.
Each housemaster was judged almost entirely by the
success of his house in the games we played and it
follows therefore that the success one had with one's
housemaster was in direct ratio to one's ability with
a leather ball.

Under the housemaster, the District Leader, came
the boys, the population, who paid or their parents
paid good money to get this. The housemaster
delegated minor authority, discipline, to four or
five top boys or prefects who could use a common
room of their own and whose perquisite it was to
send the younger boys on any errand they wanted
run. In theory these prefects elected themselves,
in practice the housemaster had his say about
elections. Any District Leader worth his salt is
careful about his District Councils. And these
District Councils, or collections of prefects in the
houses, the duties of which were inquisitorial, were
the people to keep in with. It was a humane
concentration camp.

I believe the whole system of government in Germany is founded on that evolved through centuries at the greater British public schools. At my first academy we might have been the tribes, our old tyrant our god, father and master, but when we moved on we dropped into a newer republic with a benevolent President at its head and at the other end, five despots to see we were to grow as like them as we could.

There was of course far more liberty here than at the school I had left. Later when I went on to Oxford there was more liberty again, our education seems rightly to be an advance towards the time when we have our days to arrange for ourselves, when we are to sit idly by, waiting for the clock to strike on Sunday afternoons. There was probably more liberty at this public school than at any other, we had more free time and later, when we had passed the School Certificate examination we were allowed to specialize in a single subject. In my case this meant I had hardly any work to do at all the last two years before I went to Oxford. I did nearly all my general reading in those two years. Opportunity of this kind must be of value because three years at Oxford is not enough. If one goes straight into an office on coming down it is not easy to read in the evenings after a tiring day and there are other distractions. All I know is that in my last two years at school and the two more at Oxford I read enough of what should be got through in order to keep an end up in conversation and however much I hated the school I shall always be grateful to the chance we were given to get our reading done.

Where at my first school we roamed in bands that is to say we were allowed no particular friends and as it seems to me now at this distance, we moved all together under one authority in the most primitive form of society known to man, here we at once had more leisure if only because we had each a room to ourselves, and this leisure split the school up more precisely into a pattern of life afterwards, more into defined divisions, the plate glass windows we no longer see because we are so used to them. Everyone of course had their classes to go to and at first they worked us hard in actual hours but we knew at once we were in a wider society because there were a thousand fresh distinctions each new boy had to learn. Within three weeks we had to know where each house was in case we should be wanted to run messages by our seniors and also the colours, that is the coloured caps worn by the school elevens and fifteen, rackets, fives, rowing, even for shooting and then the house colours worn by those who played for their houses. There were also junior school teams with colours of their own. With all this we had to be familiar as in an office one begins to pick up the names of competitors. There was this difference however that if after three weeks we did not know everything by heart we were beaten by house prefects.

One could be and was beaten for making a nuisance of oneself, for being too cock a hoop and this indeed was new. No one had been able to beat us except our old tyrant and he only did this if we had been idle or had broken one of his Old Testament commandments. To be beaten by him had a sort of shame, in a way it was welcomed for the attention one got but it was more a merited reproof than the expression of authority our prefects, the false demagogues, beat us by. Elected, as we have seen, by their predecessors but chosen in most cases by the housemaster, they had no truck with the younger boys except where they had their favourites. Like politicians they had one or two who told them what the general feeling was and this feeling, as it cannot be in the larger world outside, was feminine and entirely of personalities. What they thought of us would always be on our minds.

Fear therefore of what " they " might think was the great change, also being allowed to go some way into the town which had grown up about the school. Even then we must only walk one side of the street and in certain clothes. This did not seem strange because it was not so fantastic to have to do this as it was to have a room of our own and a town to walk in with shops at which to buy. What was terrible was everything we had to remember.

Analysing now one sees it was all due to having more free time. In this way, as hours get shorter as they will and everyone has more of the day off from his work much of what has been special to the moneyed classes, such as travel, will be common to all. In just this way by becoming public schoolboys we moved one step closer to life as we were to know it afterwards in London; we suddenly became conscious of ourselves though still at this early stage no more than as good Storm Troopers.

The favourite reported to the prefect often in the intervals of making love and what comment the great man made as he unbent, as all must, was handed on with every kind of feminine twist too bluntly put. This was known as " what everyone thinks of you." It was another and confusing standard so that you might be visited by a gang of contemporaries and be pulled about with the approval of house opinion and then be beaten for it afterwards by the prefects " for making such a bloody nuisance of yourself." None of this however went on at our house. Indeed I was in a favoured position in many ways.

My brother was head of the house, he was in Sixth Form, and was in the School cricket eleven. Heads of Houses were automatically prefects rather in the same way that blind people have to be helped at street corners; by some accident or chance they have come so far and thereby are qualified to be put in a position outside the hurly-burly. When I walked with him in the distinctive dress he was obliged to wear, his wand of office worn not carried due to his being in Sixth Form, it was a good deal to be seen beside him but it was as nothing to what it meant to trot along at his hip when he was changed and wearing his School Cap. Then indeed and only then, I have never afterwards known anything like it, one was the cynosure of all eyes.

Success at school is more complete than any other kind at any other time. When we see a famous man on his way through Kensington Gardens we may know or may have heard how unhappily he is married or how dreadful his life is. We may simply disagree with his views. At school, at any rate for the first two years one looked up to creatures who by their skill had got into one of the worth while teams as mythological figures, as real leaders whose glance, if it fell on one, was something in which one could take proper pride. They had no private lives, they had no views, they must be happy. They were there to make runs.

But I was more fortunate still because of an unprecedented thing, I had tea every day with my brother. As you know each boy had a separate room but the money our parents paid to keep us did not include a fire every night. Every other night we had a fire in our own grate, every alternate evening we could sit with the person who had tea with us and who, it was so arranged, could light his the night our own was cold. Tea was the only meal we had in our rooms and we were allowed to cook eggs and so on for ourselves. We were obliged while we were juniors to cook for the older boys. So it came about that every other evening when I had no fire I could sit with my brother and what cooking I did was for the two of us. I was helped at that by several other little boys because my brother was so important he had a number marked off to look after him alone.

You may think it natural for a brother to do what he did, it may seem more natural the older and more important he might be that he should do what he could for his younger brother, but if you think this you must remember that our society at school was primitive. We apologized for blood relationships, they had no place and that Gerald should remember them at a time, as everyone thought, when he must be preoccupied even all through the winter with being in the cricket eleven, was like the eccentricity of a seventeenth-century Emperor of China as one reads of it after a day's telephoning at the office. Our teas therefore came to be accepted not without scandal and without other brothers even attempting to do the same. It was a seven days' wonder which persisted and for which I was duly beaten a year later, the first day of the new term after he had gone up to Cambridge.

95

The School colours were gaudy and if in his last term, as did not often happen, we went off down the street together through shade of elm after elm along a low wall to look for old books in a second-hand shop because my brother bought numbers of these, I walked by his side elevated and in a confusion of delight, talking much too fast. Nothing could be more drab than the clothes I wore with the cap on my head which meant I played for no team at all or rather that I had not been given my colours for anything, not even the most junior team. Nothing in that term could exceed the glory of his dress, except for ten others, different even in the cricket boots he had on from anything worn by anyone else. As we went forward in the dust, the smell of exhausts, it might be on a Saturday when parents had come down, each little group had my brother pointed out and his glorious clothes explained as we went along that side of the street where only he could walk and, if he went, could take me. Windows caught the sun and boys, running through low doorways out of shops, were for the instant blinded before they saw. They would go on laughing until that other brightness of his clothes eclipsed them into a silence which became scandalized the moment they could pick me out. Even masters were different and showed themselves affable.

Gerald had another distinction. He had been elected by the time I am writing to a sort of club the prefects had amongst themselves, an institution more exclusive than any we know today, the clubroom as much a holy of holies as the old tyrant's study, a really chosen race of men which had no counterpart. They too had certain distinctions in their dress and it was their right and only theirs to take friends not so distinguished on that side of the street which it so happened was the sunny side. As we went over the bridge we both thought of fishing although there were no fish to catch, and then I might see another Son of Heaven coming towards us on our pavement. When Gerald stopped and they spoke naturally to each other my day was made. Whenever he took me off with him I hoped and hoped this would happen again.

Until he went up to Cambridge I was sheltered and could always find sanctuary in his room which meant I had more time to read and that means literally, in the hunger for reading anything and everything which began about then, I had more time to give to what became a preoccupation. Also I was spared the terror I got to know afterwards when there was that thunder of feet down the corridor and one sat still as a rabbit wondering if they were coming for one. Later at Oxford, where I had rooms over cloisters paved in stone which echoed, they would tear screaming in by either of its entrances drunk like fiends about one in the morning and, unpopular as ever, I had again to face the fact they might be after me as five years previously they had been; different, desperate now, estranged.

That last term of his my brother, who had been in the eleven three years, began to lose his form so much that in the end he lost his place. By seniority he should have been captain but at the beginning of the season they put someone else in that position and made him vice captain. He could not score runs and after each failure I used to go about in selfconscious apprehension, dismayed to this extent that I could not bring myself ever to mention the subject to him. When the blow fell and they printed the lists of those to play in the last all important match, he had been dropped but they did not leave his name out altogether, they put it in brackets under the name of the captain. This fact by inference gives an idea of how seriously everyone felt on a matter of games. These became affairs of honour, corporate duels in which everyone tried to take a part, or failing this, took an exclusive interest. When we knew he would not play people went out of their way to be kind. It was terrible and the glory reflected becoming so much less actually gave me a sense of shame.

But the shaming thing, however natural it might be at such a time, was that one should take so much pleasure in being known to the successful, that if one could not rise to the heights of the eleven, if one could not straddle the top of Everest the next best thing was to be known to those who could and did. It is the yard stick of our fatuity to realize that to nearly all the younger boys this attitude was inevitable and the recognized standard by which their position in the school was judged. Much no doubt was due to fear, to a desire to obtain protection and this aspect may explain the revolt which took place the day peace was declared.

I was in my first term and was going off to get some more to eat when I saw the headmaster about to read from a typescript to a small crowd of boys at a place in front of the library where nothing was ever read to us. I took to my heels and was in time to hear of the Armistice. I felt as though someone had taken a pile of blankets off me and with a great feeling of unrest began to run again. We nearly all of us ran the rest of that day.

Now it so happened there was in that hyper-exclusive club of prefects I have mentioned one who was thought to be a German and the club had been criticized for electing a Hun. In spite of his position he had because of this fact led a leper's sort of life while the war was on. It was he who organized the riot that evening. At the head of us all he called for the master who was in command of the Officers' Training Corps to show himself at a window. This our Colonel did and took his chance to announce that he would resign immediately. When he said this we all thought authority was at an end with the war. We were out of hand in a moment, the whole school stayed out after hours without permission, we broke windows, we cheered, we bought flags and fireworks, we assaulted a master and when we were so well away that the great men sallied forth from their clubroom to keep order we turned on our heroes and chased them back inside again. In doing this, the most natural thing in the world as it seems today, we showed then that we were mad. The odd thing is that when we were ourselves again, no one was genuinely sorry. What we had done was a sign of the times, proof that boys, without knowing or even wanting it, will sometimes turn like worms.

We may have revolted against fear but it is more likely we thought for once the world was ours who were so young we did not have to mourn the dead, who did not guess the price we in our turn might have to pay for other boys to celebrate the victory by, that which our lives must buy today sooner than tomorrow, no doubt to turn the worms again.

WHILE my brother was still at school I was in a sheltered position; as soon as he left I was beaten for it. At the same time I passed an examination by which I ceased to be a junior, that is I no longer had to run messages for prefects or to cook their teas. And so another phase began.

We had more leisure, we began to have time to look about and make friends. Those who had played in the junior cricket or football elevens were marked out, they were in favour with the house prefects. One of them played so well he was in our house eleven while still a junior. The effect on him was curious for it gave him dignity even when he was not wearing his cap, like a king bare-headed. He was not conceited but he was remote because of his skill and very good-looking with long eyelashes. He spoke slow, was probably intensely stupid. He was tolerant, he could afford to be and so took everything calmly. By contrast the rest of us were maniacs.

Those who had been in one of the junior house elevens were keen enough and some of those who just made up sides were keener still, not only at games but on whether individuals were " awful."

In our house there was a form of public conscience based on opinions categorically laid down in the form of principles. These were on no account defined and seldom told to the offender's face so that if one had been what " they " called " awful " one knew of it by a sort of studied rudeness the more boring because it laid no claim to wit.

There was little physical violence, the only bullying was of one poor boy who was so religious he knelt down in the passage and prayed every time the prefects were going to beat him. No one could be blamed for knocking him about, he had twice been known literally to turn the other cheek. Public opinion could have no effect because he was taken up with God. The prefects beat him for being obsessed, it was no concern of theirs what occupied his every waking thought. The rest of us bullied him because it was intolerable it should be God.

The opinions in the light of which they judged us were laid down by the prefects and varied with individuals in some respects; as they left those who replaced them were more or less fanatical than their predecessors and in this way opinion in the house changed. The middle part of the house, that is the majority who were neither junior nor senior, interpreted what they thought the prefects felt and rubbed it in. They did this, which is the horrible thing, not from a belief that the standard they considered they were set was best for the house or by extension for the school but generally because by professing a faith they thought their seniors held they hoped to advance their own condition, to become initiates.

We were beginning to be too old or too well established now to curry favour for self-protection, we did it out of a love or respect for conventions which would get us on and which had no counterpart in after life except in so far as any convention serves to make life easier by levelling inequalities. Thus when I began to rebel and bought a greatcoat which was longer than it might have been, it came down below the knee, I broke no rule of school dress any more than the Guards officer who goes to Lord's to watch cricket in a soft collar transgresses Army Regulations. I was not beaten for it but for some time was not allowed to forget.

If we were too conventional there was this advantage that any boy who felt he must break away had to face opposition and there was enough to daunt any but the determined. Boys are exhibitionists, too much licence and the school no doubt would have been a crazy place but the system as known to me meant that it was applied by toadies to their own ends. This to such a degree that one suspected any criticism first as being spying and secondly a means by which the spy hoped to advance himself with prefects.

What we felt about the prefects was felt by them about those who had been elected to the prefects' club, no doubt the ordinary masters took pains to keep on the right side of housemasters, there was even a kind of society between their wives but we heard no more than rumblings of this as when at home the quarries were blasting fifteen miles off along the Malvern Hills. And while it was horrible enough there were reversals of fortune even to those who worked hardest for the system because any kind of keenness except at games was frowned on by the boys, the prefects and unofficially by the masters.

When anyone toadied to such an extent he began not to be human, and toadying alters the expression of the face in extreme cases, the prefects showed displeasure which was taken up at once by the rest of us so that it was even safe to say as I went by " my God, Jones, you are awful." Care had to be taken however, these reversals could be short. If one did not know that Jones or Smith was back in " their " favour, one was liable to pay for it.

This system of applied conventions extended naturally to the furniture. We found a wallpaper of trellised roses, a bed, a writing table and bookcase over it both of which could be locked with keys which opened every other boy's table in the house, it was all of a pattern even to the keys, a small grate, a small window and an easy chair with a sort of hard mattress in red material. There must also have been a table to have tea on, I forget, but one's clothes went in drawers which were a part of the writing-desk.

All the wood was varnished black and had lumps knocked out and names cut in. We could hang pictures on the walls, but not every picture.

There was a lady who did watercolours every day and all day of the principal school buildings. She sold them for six or eight guineas. If we had the money we could have them in our rooms; it was not encouraged but it was not thought " awful." By far the greater number of pictures were those which had been left behind by boys when they went up to the Universities. There were sporting prints, of steeple-chasing, men shooting over dogs in old-fashioned clothes with blunderbusses and most of all globular partridges each hair on each feather carefully drawn and more globular pheasants done the same but with long tails. Of course there were others with hounds in full cry and even one or two, aiming high, of sheep at sunset on snow covered ground under Scotch firs but generally on going into a room you would be met by dull red eyes looking out of masses of khaki feathers. The glass might be broken, in some frames there would be no glass at all and throughout the afternoon at any time of year the window would be open.

If I was by chance almost alone in the house at about this period I used to run round shutting all the windows to annoy the matron who would open them without thinking as other people pick their noses. And it was about now, to annoy the others, that I hung some pictures of my own.

I had a number of lithographs of old buildings in Tewkesbury modestly framed, drawings of the antique black and white buildings to be seen there with, in each foreground, an old countrywoman perhaps, dressed in the fashions of two hundred years ago. These figures were put in to show how respectable the houses were; they were so ancient, so picturesque they could have been taken for brothels in Normandy resorts and it was probably the costumes, of about the same date as those others out shooting or being run away with after hounds hung in almost every other room that saved mine from being smashed. Later, daring, I added some small, hideous Mexican bird pictures done with brilliantly coloured feathers and even they survived. But when, out of exhibitionism no doubt, I added the horse's hat there was mild trouble of a sort.

It was a wide round hat of plaited straw. In the middle, where it would come over the sharp-edged forehead horses have as all know who have been struck over the nose when riding, it had a little witch's point, a cone which stood up to insulate the horse's head from sun. This hat was like those which some years later girls wore to sun-bathe in only there were two holes cut on either hand for those upstanding horse's ears with fur inside, the cuckolds.

This horse's sunbonnet is the extent of my emancipation at that time. Not having drawn enough attention by exhibiting pictures of old houses I had tried the curiosity of bird pictures. When this failed, and I suppose things brought back from abroad if not too big got by in spite of being " awful," I had gone for this odd hat which I had painted in alternate rings of red and yellow.

Can anything more ridiculous be imagined ? You may think I wore it to be conspicuous but I cannot remember ever doing this, it hung on a nail and was as pointless as any act in that age of exquisite pointlessness, when all there is to do is to grow up.

We began then to have more time to make friends and there was a set I was half in with. It had two members who were intimate with the house prefects as far as they could be at our age and these two boys, both of them good at games, were our leaders. They were our leaders, that is we looked to them for our own advancement.

There was also the housemaster. He came round every evening when we were in bed, we began to get to know him. He had complete control of our fortunes, in other words he could have us sacked and in many houses the housemaster kept control over the attitude adopted by the prefects. Ours was not popular enough to influence opinion and he never got rid of me because I kept within the law, nor have I any cause to think he wanted me out of his house. But I think he hated me and I knew I hated him. This intense dislike made any success I might have had the more unlikely. I needed praise badly, and if

I had had it might be even less of a person now, but from the lack of it at that time found everything pointless, so blind that no effort at work or play ever seemed worth while.

There were several of us at this stage not good enough at games to distinguish ourselves and not encouraged to show we were keen at anything else. One, who had a room near mine, expressed himself by having slightly exaggerated clothes, in particular his collars had long points. These peculiarities, as in the small differences there may be in suits made by the best London tailors—slight enough to be impossible for women to notice without having them pointed out, were so technical that only boys who had been more than one year at school could appreciate them. He was dirty, had a raffish look about him, and was malicious with a lisp.

I simply cannot remember much more of it all in detail but I rely on what I cannot forget, the every day feeling I had at that time. It may be this is imagination. On the other hand I had begun to keep a diary part of which has survived and this gives exactly that sensation of being watched and of oneself keeping track of even simple actions for the reactions these might bring on the part of house opinion. It follows therefore that my greatcoat which I got probably under the influence of my friend, and the sunbonnet, which was carrying the coat a step further, were the pathetic motions made by the unsuccessful to attract notice to a negligible personality. At the same time, because we and a few like us were no good at games and so there was nothing else for us to do but rebel, they were feminine motions.

We were feminine not from perversion, although it is true that we were preoccupied by sex, but from a lack of any other kind of self expression. Also we watched the effect we produced on others in the way women do and this on account of the system under which the general opinion held of us had a disproportionate effect upon our security and in consequence upon our peace of mind. But whatever reasons we might have we screamed and shrieked rather than laughed and took a sly revenge rather than having it out with boxing gloves as parents will still imagine.

I heard my friend next door had sent to Harrod's for itching powder which he meant to put in my shirts because I had objected to his borrowing them. I at once went to his room when he was out and slopped ink onto his walls. When he got back he came to me knowing I had done it and said he would kill the fellow who had been so frightful. But he did not ask me outright if I was the chap any more than I had bothered to ask him if he had sent for itching powder. And we neither of us relied on a row face to face to settle our differences. We looked instead to working on our two leaders with a tale of what the other had done until they pronounced that one or the other was " awful." If, as sometimes happened, they said both were " awful " then these two were cast together, friends again in that brief shipwreck such displeasure brought at school.

In such a female world much must be qualified. If the prefects beat a boy for not washing or for wearing filthy clothes the boy was admired by the majority, in fact those who were beaten most for any reason not tied with the ethic of playing games were heroes in their little way. But if one of them broke training, was caught and was beaten for it then you could safely say " Really so and so is hopeless."

The prefects themselves had a warm feeling for those they beat most. A curious thing is that those who belonged to the exclusive club were privileged to use a bamboo rod, ordinary prefects could beat only with a cane. It was respectable to be punished for being ordinarily dirty, but if you played games well it was better you should get out of hand at times not connected with cricket or football because then it made " them " think of when " they " had been a handful. And I have often wondered whether it was this which induced our headmaster at the time when I in my turn became a house prefect to make a new rule, that each prefect in a house where a boy had been caught smoking should write out a Georgic.

There was a boy who, when called by the maid in

the morning, was found propped up in bed half-way through a cigarette. She had to report him, we each had to do five hundred lines. When we had him in to put those questions one still has to ask before deciding on punishment, known as " seeing what he has to say for himself," he took up the attitude adopted by the only criminal I have met in office life. He said he did not know, that he could not think, that the whole thing was beyond him. He even refused to say whether or no he had been smoking. We did not enjoy beating as probably many prefects did but we beat him in relays as hard as we knew how. It may well be this new rule was to make us pay for our authority by writing out the lines, to suffer for what others had done as one does daily if in authority at an office. If this was the case then the effect of our suffering, and it so happened that not one of us knew enough Latin to understand Virgil, the writing out of our lines had as little connection with the offence as the effect someone's mistake will make on the profits, one's pocket, if one is paid by results and in charge of a man dealing with some technical problem that he and only he can cope with.

Our trouble was that if we came to think of it at school we could not understand. We could not make out why we did such silly things, we did not see why so much that was absurd should be done to us. When as juniors we kicked someone it was safe to kick, it was not only that we liked to give pain. It was the expression of something as altogether out of my reach then as it is now. I could not imagine then any more than I can at this moment why he chose to smoke when he must be caught. I was always confused and everything seemed pointless. Even the things we were taught in class had no reference to the life we knew we were to know.

Little girls we are told, we like to think, dream in the day of the babies they will have and, when they know about husbands, of his eyes, the colour of his hair. Boys think of sexual gratification long before they know what it is all about and before what dog-like instinct they may already have can physically be gratified. They are like dogs but girls have dolls and what forgotten tenderness is it which leads boys when very small to go to bed with teddy bears ? But we, a year or two past puberty, no dolls for us, above all no thoughts of children, imagined women as one dreams now at one's desk of a far country unvisited with all its mystery of latitude and place. If, as now, it is in spring we wonder how far on the season is, whether the leaves are out and how far on this or that blossom over the first flowering shrubs the names of which we do not know. But we wondered then ecstatically what it would be like and, not being able to avoid this wonder, as we can now dismiss things we have not seen, we fell back again and more to feeling everything was pointless.

This was the first period of adolescence, a time to

my mind that is of all the phases men go through one of the most moving because it will not be dismissed, the most alive of all his experience except when, perhaps seven years later, he high dives into love.

ON Saturday parents brought daughters down to see their brothers and, as this was a fashionable school and many of these girls if they were old enough had their photographs in the weekly papers, one knew them by sight before one was faced by what to me was beginning to be the glory of their flesh. It was time that I should begin to notice and, as I had had no contact, almost no conversation even with any but servants, and maids I did not seem to take for girls, I started at the extreme and put them on thrones, more particularly because I had been reading Keats. Nobody who has sisters can tell how remote they are to those who have none and, their appearance now being exactly what I admired, I went down the street finding angels dressed like crown princesses in every little judy visiting her brother.

When we knew someone had his sister in his room to tea we would tear down the corridor and burst into it as though we did not know he was entertaining. He would realize and so would she once the noise we made was heard; she did not have to be told any more than I do now when I go into a works where they employ female labour. He would be embarrassed and she would look up in that placid accepting way they have which hides a curiosity hungrier than ours and, when we were inside and were apologizing before we dashed out, it was our turn to be shy at her knife-like shyness buttered over with an accommodating smile. When we were gone his mother might say what noisy friends but he would have to be older than we were at that time to tease his sister with the truth which she had known at once.

It was their skin got me which I had never touched except on hands and which I thought to be softer than I afterwards found, that skin down from the neck coming out of flowering summer dresses which sent me back to my room to read Spenser. It was their eyes I never looked into I was too modest and too modest by far to fall in love, their arms which I thought were cold and which I could not think they ever used to help them kiss, their lightness I did not know the weight of, the different way they moved and literally then it seemed as though they were walking in water up over their heads along the glaring street, all this bemused me although I had been reading Herrick. For I did not believe what was written in books and when I saw there how women enjoyed making love I could not, it was too much to believe.

For years they were so beautifully far with their

kind of laughter and their way of talking that I
thought the one approach was by conversation and
from this I was debarred by the animal mystery they
held of bearing life within them. It could as I had
come to know be shared in part by men but not so
far as I could think by myself. I had yet to learn anyone would look at the figure I cut then talking too fast
as I had at my brother's elbow in the glory of his
special clothes, pestering any girl I got to know later
with excited chatter on an indifferent subject just
because I was at her side. I was in love with love
and could not bring this back to individuals so that
when I thought of fornication it was of a marriage
with sympathetic swans in an element like the air I
could not fly in and was half a stranger to.

As many of these girls were figures in the outside
world, and, in consequence, were discussed by people
who did not know them, we came to hear of their
peculiarities. One sister who was often down to see
her brother was fond, or so it was said, of kissing.
When I saw her after I had heard this, I thought
she was a prostitute, it seemed so horrible that she
could like it. Some time later when I learned they
wore nothing under their evening dresses I almost
fainted. Two mothers were talking and they agreed
it was unfair on young men for their daughters to
wear so little. I did not dare to disagree and besides
I was so sure girls entirely ignored me I was pro-
foundly grateful for any such evidence they were

girls that I might have dancing, however shared. But this was much later and if I had been told at the time I should have been disgusted.

Indeed anything in too much detail was revolting, so much so that women bathing and coming out of the water in their wet suits seemed very far from those objects of delight we saw on calendars, chocolate boxes or the films. What we had read in England's Helicon was remote but closer to us than the breath of living which we knew as little of as those who, never travelling on the Tube, know of straphanging from what they can smell on top of the moving stairs. We lived in a confusion of desire like one who sees his cake but cannot have it and so were better off than boys at co-educational schools. What we most wanted at that time was someone in authority whose praise was worth working for and something to dream of in between. If we could not by accident have the praise nothing could keep us off the mystery of sex except a glut of girls about us which by good fortune, or a wise choice, we escaped.

In one house which overlooked another a boy could see into a maid's room across the way and she did not draw the blinds when she undressed. Night after night long after he should have been in bed he sat up till half-past ten and every night she went to bed of course, taking off her clothes to do it. Their windows were some way apart, there was almost nothing he could make out except the glint of flesh but it worked on him to this extent that he had to go away for the whole of one term to rest. And yet, if he had been closer, if she had undressed in his room, he would almost certainly have been appalled. He may have realized this because he never tried to get to know her.

I myself spent hours at my window one summer when there was an epidemic in the house opposite because a trained nurse had been put in a boy's room and on the hotter nights I hoped she would not draw her blind. I watched as does a cat which has not yet caught a mouse sitting over an old hole expecting at every minute. But it was no good and now that I have read novels of hospital life I know the medical students must have made her careful.

The authorities were alive to this. The maids who did our rooms were chosen for their elderly bad looks. They kept the keys on the inside of their locks for their rooms were on the corridors along with ours. Mine was called Dinge. She was very thin with pale-blue eyes almost as white and pale as her sparse untidy hair. I never saw her when she was not worried because she was kind. Her face was thin with a hooked nose you felt you could see through against a light and her name miraculously expressed her in the way nicknames do at school.

Once when I was washing up in the pantry opposite I heard a crash from her room and running across put my ear to the keyhole. She had smashed her wash-basin and when she began wailing out to herself what she had done and how she had had it these twenty years, I called one or two others up. We listened entranced, we were not very pleasant in those days.

It was overdone the way we spied on everything, then on each other, our curiosity had no bounds but it was natural enough where women were concerned. Mine was so great I remember telling as a piece of news that I had seen one of the masters come by outside smoking his pipe after hours, that is when they could not have met one of the boys because they were not supposed to smoke in front of us. Also, on a summer half-holiday, when I was running back for one of the roll calls they held to prevent us going too far out of bounds if we had escaped a game, I came blind round a corner slap into the arms of a girl. She had put her hands out to save herself but my rush carried me past them and so for the first time I was into someone's arms. After apologizing I went away dazed for this then was what it must be like, this softness like a tight bolster and over her chest some sort of shirt covered with starched frills which had pricked my chin. I told no one and, come to that, have never told anyone before.

This watching, this spying through keyholes, so furtive as it seems now must not be thought furtive at the age we were then. In certain conditions of life it is taken as inevitable and as a natural form of

self-expression. Thus when I was home for the summer holidays and took a book which I did not read
up on that hill which overlooked Tewkesbury and
the river and from which, down on my right, I could
see the ferry where my boat was tied, there was
on the other side a bathing-place. A disused railway
carriage had been put there to undress in but the
girls did not use it and took off their clothes behind
withies which lined most of that bank. I had not
come to read and they had not come to take off their
things unseen. On the other hand I was too far off,
although I could well have sat much closer, to see
details and in any case they were experts in slipping
on one garment under another or whatever it was
they did. But they dressed and undressed more or
less in the open for the fun of being overlooked by
those on their own side and they knew I was up on
the hill opposite because when they were spied on by
a boy in their own territory and they crept round to
my side of their withy to avoid this they shrieked at
my distant figure, tickled to death. Here then was an
accepted way for them to get through an afternoon
and not one I need have been ashamed of as I was
at the time. Bodies should be objects of curiosity and
it is a comment on the way we were brought up that
we should find them exciting because forbidden. At
the same time I would not have it any other way.
Sex is the great stimulus and it was not only that but
a great mystery as well in those days, without which

a boy could have gone through school and not have
read a single book outside of his lessons. There
should come a time for boys to wait up over windows
and it should be forbidden them, to give that encouragement which makes it worth their while.

It is not only sex, which he is not allowed, drives
him to look about him, but the everyday conventions of a school are of value to anyone strong or
unhappy enough to stand up to the disapproval dislike of them brings. What he comes to learn of how
the opinion in his house will react to conduct which
does not run along with its own will help him to get
by long after he has left, indeed until sooner or
later he no longer cares what people think. When
they say that going to a public school trains one to
come naturally into a room full of strangers they also
mean it teaches some boys with two eyes how to deal
with an assembly of one-eyed people with a squint.
He learns when they face him that they may not
see him at all but when they are sideways and their
faces aslant then probably they are not thinking of
themselves and may be dangerous.

Again by having sex put out of reach he gets the
benefit of an exaggerated outlook on it. When I was
rowing up the river to fish by the weir and I had to
go past that bathing-place, I always rowed fast. It
was partly out of modesty because I did not think
they would want to be bothered with my getting too
near. If I had tied my boat under their bank they

might soon have had enough and in consequence no longer have played their little game when I was up on the hill. But I would also hurry past because I was shy of such facts as those girls exemplified. Shy from innocence no doubt but surely shyness is the saving grace in all relationships, the not speaking out, not sharing confidences, the avoidance of intimacy in important things which makes living, if you can find friends to play it that way, of so much greater interest even if it does involve a lot of lying.

It was this shyness, more than innocence, and the fact that I could not stop talking which first led me at this period to lie outrageously when in the company of strangers. I could not help myself in railway carriages, and it took a form so obviously extravagant and false that I could never hope I should be believed. Coming up to London the line passed a vast dump of discarded Army lorries on what is now a Trading Estate. I had been talking to those in the carriage all the way from Reading and now I told them I had been employed (and I was obviously fifteen) in reconditioning these lorries. At this an elderly man opposite could stand no more and to silence me asked how much I thought it would cost to put one right. I remember exactly I said it would depend upon the condition of the lorry, elaborated this and ended by putting forward my estimate of £100. He grunted. I found afterwards I was not far out and was so pleased.

Another time I was coming home for the holidays in one of those slow trains which, on their way to Cheltenham, stop at every station along the Cotswolds and are so leisurely you can take part in the country while you go. There was no corridor to the carriage and at one small station a girl got in. I was alone and was at once tremendously embarrassed, her being there made me wonder if she thought I was thinking not of pouncing on her, that was too far off even to imagine at that period, but of bothering her with conversation. I looked hard out of the window. It was a smoking compartment and she made some movement which made me turn to her. She was taking out a cigarette. At that date this was tolerably daring. She said, " I do hate men who smoke shag in carriages, don't you ? " and I hastily agreed. I remember no more, it is my mood at that moment I can feel now and it was a lying mood. I have no doubt I told her all sorts of stories and kept my distance.

These things last because of the shy hunger I had then to talk to everyone I met and especially to girls if someone else were present. It did not matter who, man or woman, but so long as I was not alone with a person I had to display myself. She was the first strange girl I had talked to alone for I was at that time one of those who speak more loudly than they need to a companion while seeking out with their eyes sidelong what effect their conversation has on others present. In this way horses clumsily pretend to crop the grass as they draw closer.

I had not yet found the Robinson Crusoe in two people temporarily islanded by their exchanges, lying no doubt but always with half-truths like truffles just under the surface for one or the other to turn up to find the inkling of what human beings treasure, rather than what they think they know of themselves. I never fell in love while I was at school and it was not till later when I got to know others more of my type outside the house that I had any private exchange of ideas or expression of feelings. At this time when those of us who were of the same age met in each other's rooms we were still in that primitive condition we had been at our first schools and we used to go about in bands. Thus our talk was directed generally into the room for the approval of those present and not in any one direction though it may well have been aimed. Not yet had we had that exchange with another about the wide world, which we thought would prove a paradise because we were ambitious and unhappy. Once we had escaped and left we never thought we should think of this time again. We never guessed our thoughts would be driven back to it, that we might have to die not so long after we came to be old boys, before enough had happened to drive all recollection of it out, if so much is ever forgotten.

As likely as not when we gathered together in a

room at this period we would discuss one of the
manifestations of our adolescence, the interminable
thieving we suffered. No one was safe and in due
course two boys were asked not to come back. They
had no connection with each other, each stole
separately, all they had in common was that both
took money.

We played the detective, trying to work out where
everyone was when the money must have gone. We
did not find this stealing criminal or " awful " in
the sense that it was bad for the house. We should
have been harder on whoever it was if he had taken
the cups the house had won at games to melt them
down although we could not afford to have our
pocket money stolen from us, all those strawberries
sugar and cream. At the same time we never
deposited our cash with the matron who would have
kept it locked away and I think this was because no
one wanted her to know how much he had got in
case she told the others. Instead there were some who
kept their money locked in their bureaus although
they knew any key would open theirs while others
put the notes behind picture frames and then in any
general discussion admitted where they were hidden
although the thief might have been in the room.

We did not go the length another housemaster did,
for there was any amount of theft throughout the
school, who put a pin through the king's eye where
it was printed on a note and left this out to be stolen.

We were in all several hundred boys and I suppose the greater number of us knew of it, the shopkeepers told us they had been warned to look for a pinhole in the eye. Nor for that matter did we have a boy set fire to the building as happened at one academy where he was caught setting light to bundles of newspapers in a passage. At our place it was only money was taken and when in the end they were supposed to have been caught and were asked not to return we thought their lives had been ruined. In point of fact it made no permanent difference to them whatever, neither I am sure has ever taken anything again. It is some spring fever in the long spring of adolescence, it may be the wish to be daring which made me hang up the sunbonnet on my wall, a first attempt to break out which made them do it. In this way we were right not to think this kind of theft " awful," but for the wrong reasons. Everything was topsy turvy.

Now there began for me a time of great unhappiness while I was trying to unravel everything and which led me into a kind of extravagant behaviour.

AFTER my brother left my horizon was bounded by the two boys who were our leaders because they played football for the house in spite of being so young. One was lazy and good-looking, different even when he did not wear his cap, his colours as we called it; the other was fairheaded and big, a waspish nature, capricious in his moods. He could not be trusted when he pretended to despise the cult of games and was in those days essentially a feminine character, the reverse of what he seemed. We revolved around these two suns and kept quite successfully out of trouble with the prefects.

As time went on the set we made began to break up. Once started this movement was gradual but painful so far as I was concerned. One or two became sixteen years of age, they were beginning to be old gentlemen, they would be leaving after two or three more years. They began to make friends outside the house and accidentally enough no doubt, although it was to haunt me for some time to come, they got in with the successful in some instances or suddenly developed skill at a game like fives.

Fives courts are three sided, built of stone, plain

high walls open to the sky and on the left wall what is known as a pepperbox which is a low projection into the court up to one's shoulder, topped by an ecclesiastical moulding. The game was first played so they say at Eton when boys knocked about with a ball between two buttresses on the outside of the School Chapel. You wear padded gloves on each hand and hit the ball with these keeping a loose wrist. There is the service which is guileless, a fierce return of service crack crack crack quick as a rattle round the three sides of the court and then the rally. When four people play the game there are shouts of " mine."

Our courts were built in a long row back to back and when my hour's exercise was done I used to drift along them. More and more often my friends played with strangers in friendly games. Each house had three or four courts allotted to it but they would play away from our own. I had not even heard they intended playing and this showed how out of their lives I could be that I did not share their plans. I did not like to stop to watch for fear they might think I was trying to get to know the others. When I saw them that evening in the house I would say meaningly " I saw you playing fives today " and as they could see nothing odd in this they would hardly bother to answer. I thought they were evasive and the next time in the School Shop, which was by the fives courts, I would stand by the door to

see if any of them were with their new friends. If
they were then I would go away.

One term I could hardly keep away from these
courts. The game collected all those I knew into
a coverable space, I could keep my eye on what I
now felt was their escape and my dwindling security.
I began not to feel safe for it is fatal to stay any time
alone at school and rather than make up to those
in the house younger than myself I saw that I must
look outside.

Behind the line of courts built back to back was a
single row so that there was a walk with fives being
played on both sides, right and left. A fives court
is twelve foot across. Walking between you could
go from one foursome to the next, so fast from one
quick game to another in which friends might be
engaged with couples strange to you but not to them.
Now he who takes service, crouching behind the
pepperbox to make his return, is out of sight so that
in each court you could see only three players at a
glance. We were so shy, it was almost slyness, not
to be found watching in case our friends should think
we were trying to get on terms with theirs that every
four paces we had to glance quickly left and right
to see if there were any we knew playing. Then we
had to watch for the fourth player to come out in
the rallies as our friends were now on such terms
that one had been known to play with three
strangers.

It would have been friendly to stand by a game to praise the play thus getting to know the players strange to us. In this way we could have risen on our friends' shoulders and moved with them in those wider circles which were opening. But some snub forgotten now or an inability to get on with those I did not know because I tried to overimpress warned me so that what should have been natural and easy in both senses seemed impossible, too friendly, and a base way of making up to people more fortunate.

A suspicious nature is mean and I became convinced my friends did not take up with new people to have fun but to get on, to be more popular than they were which was a thing I affected to despise. I could not see that whatever they might do outside the house was more natural than the competition for favour existing within it by which most of us struggled to improve our chances to become prefects in or before our turn. The ambitious gained little by knowing strangers, it could only help later when they were prefects and hoped to be elected to the prefects club. But I found it sinister, was always down by the fives courts spying out, and so dropped further away deflated, thinking they soared.

The sun slanted up in the sky threw shadows from the sidewalls of those courts. I walked between through shadows recurring in triangles, out into the sun then back into shade, slinking as I was with jealousy in a scene animated by the activity of the game. It is the most abstract of all to watch except billiards, the court a threesided box open above and at the back, the low wall shoulder high jutting out decorated at its top when all else is plain and flat, the three players with their bunched gloves and then the fourth cracked out, a friend suddenly revealed, who could the others be, his shout of " mine," my dash into the next tooth of shade and the next game. As they played they pranced always throwing their arms out to hit and I learned jealousy beyond anything I had felt at an extra favour shown my brothers at home.

This was no display of love, I was in love with love with no conception of love. It was a feeling others were doing better, it was something everyone was to know much later in London, the pang on hearing someone else has been to a gay party, that feeling well here is proof we are dropping out. It was social and particularly at that time linked with security because to lag behind at school, to lose contact, is to run the risk of more than loneliness, to be ragged because one is the sort of person who would be lonely, to be mobbed by rooks.

Loneliness began for me now fierce, desperate, taking on an importance out of all proportion to its quality which was that of a boy in his 'teens who thought he was too good for pleasures not shared in conversation. The exchange to be had in games, boring enough no doubt, the "good shot" the "well played" dull as they are but still appreciation expressed, and we all needed praise, these I did not want to have through joining in an exercise.

Another trouble was the question of titles. The peculiar snobbery at this school was that at roll calls Honourables were prefixed Mister when they had their names read out and the Marquis of So and So was named in full instead of plain Lord So. Now I was a title snob. As soon as I realized this, when I had burst into tears twelve months earlier on not being able to go to stay with a noble, I fought it and through fighting had come to think everyone at this school suffered but that they did not fight as I did. For years I struggled until much later I could say that no sort or kind of title made any difference. I thought currying favour with those good at games was bad enough but as nothing to making up to peers, all the more so because I could not say why it should be dreadful. Playing compulsory football against another junior house eleven I insulted one harmless count by calling him a "belted earl." This was naturally considered "awful" and I began to have delusions of persecution. I came upon one of my friends playing fives with three peers, owing to the war there were plenty at this school, and went back to my house quite certain such treachery must have its punishment later in some blow of fate. I felt so strongly I have no idea today if there was really the amount of snobbery I smelled out there. However absurd I only know it made me miserable.

These were the days when to be alone was to feel one had escaped for the moment not from any overt bullying but from what appeared to be the threat. There was a strain in trying to keep up with new friendships which probably did not exist. There was the dread of going into a friend's room to find one was not wanted, to be abandoned by the two leaders now that they were too busy to bother and worst of all the self questioning as to why this should be, the fear it might be a peer or one of the school's racquet players and of what this meant if true. The best was to get away in those few hours we had on our own, to chance being seen lonely in the effort to forget.

It may have been a cricket match which finished early or a public holiday when we were allowed to watch the school eleven playing or to wander off where we liked, but I went down to the river by myself and watched for fish, and crouched by a tree in the wordless almost ecstatic state a sort of release from misery brings at that age I found two swans floating past locked in a fight or love I did not know, their necks entwined one head fastened on the other, both half drowned with barely beating wings.

Another time across the river an old lady sat in a low chair with her knees, over where her feet rested on the ground, rather above the level of her middle. Suddenly she slipped off till she squatted on the grass her bottom jammed up against her heels and her back against the chair. She could not get up. She began to let out one curious weak cry after another, distress is exactly the word.

Again perhaps one of a master's flapper daughters would ride haughty by in pigtails and I would be ashamed again to be seen alone. Or the headmaster himself whom I knew and who took me riding sometimes and I would wonder, not caring, whether he would stop.

All this is so far now and yet there is in these chance escapes almost any summer day at any time of life if one is off alone and particularly in country where one grew up. Then it is almost impossible not to remember adolescence, the imminent feeling that soon everything will be made known.

But I should give an altogether false idea of my time at school by describing it as one long moaning and groaning. There were things anyone could do. He could get away by himself in the winter terms by going out with the beagles. There was a pack of these nearby we were allowed to run after and an afternoon following them counted as the hour's exercise each one of us had to mark against his name on the notice board. This turned out to be my game of fives by which to make friends, possibly because I was so short of breath with hour after hour of running that it was impossible to insist on talk as the first step to friendship.

The country we hunted was flat, large fields of stubble, wire fences and any number of hares so that when one of these got tired another was put up. We ran and ran drawn out into a long line, panting, kept apart from those near us by the thumping heart, the lungs which could not spare a breath for speech. The beagles' sides went out and in, small bellows to bring out their cry and soon they ran silent. The hare, always fresh, never the one we had hunted in the last endless field, leapt out of sight in male ballet dancer bounds, forever seeming to look back at us as jockeys will when away in front not far from the post.

We hardly ever killed or if we did I do not remember it. Once a great friend I made in this, and he is my friend to this day, running with me off the line, as we made for a rick of straw behind which we hoped to have a smoke, pointed out a labourer trotting round. He would stoop every now and again to throw a stone. When we came up we saw it was a hunted hare too tired to do more than go in small circles. As we reached him he killed it.

I remember I laughed as those negroes laughed on the banana boat at New Orleans when years later I was going to Vera Cruz. They were running round an open hatch hurling lumps of coal down at other negroes below and out of sight in the ship's hold. They had begun with small pieces and then, as the joke had grown on them they had chosen larger blocks until they were throwing lumps so big they had to use two hands to lift. When their friends climbed out covered with blood which showed no more than water on their skins they all ran off down the dock howling with laughter.

Through laughing and cursing together and through the complicity of smoking cigarettes with comparative strangers I made friends who opened a new kind of life I had had no idea went on. Now for our hour's exercise we were allowed, if not picked for football, to go for a run as far as we liked so long as it was in a certain direction. I did not know people ever went further than the outskirts of the school but I was to find how wrong I was, being as usual one of the last to know.

As early as possible we would set out on October afternoons loping past the place where the older boys we were to become next summer were allowed to bathe. Here we should lie naked watching on the racecourse opposite jockeys take their horses by, and the sun which was to play over us would sharpen all the colours they wore as they watched each other at this point which was the furthest from the puny stands. But now in this weather under one of those highest skies of blue above long fish skeletons of cloud, across the white stubble flat as bones which scrunched at each reach our feet made, leaving that bathing place behind we were soon up to the pence coloured oasis the sewage farm in its encouragement to vegetation contributed in autumn to those tow-headed fields. Ten minutes later and we would be past some bungalows and then had arrived at our gravel pit. It had been dug out of the ground and on such a day as this was a shallow depression gold in the pale plain and built up in the middle a donkey engine in a cab, purple and black, to draw tubs on rails up the ramp to the gravel washing plant all red with rust.

None but ourselves came near and we at once lit up forbidden cigarettes. Our idea at one time was to raise steam in the broken plant but we never knew how to get water into the boiler. We argued there must already be water·in it and lit fires only to put these out for fear the whole thing might blow up. Accordingly we had to push the tubs up by hand to crash them by letting them go careering down the ramp. When we grew tired of this we lay back in our white and blue caps on the heaped golden pebbles blowing the smoke we inhaled up to where a mile high there drifted identically coloured bones of cloud picked white by waves now stilled of that blue air. We could not often go to this place and when we did it was as if to an assignation, a lost world stretching back to the time we were children and had a corner in the shrubbery which we had made ours, behind where Poole used to burn dead leaves.

One day soon after I had first been to this gravel

pit and as I sat smoking with the others who happened not to be members of my house, what seemed to be a young man rode up on an expensive motorbike. He was helmeted and wore goggles. When he took these off I recognized a boy rather younger than myself from the same house. I had no notion he did this on his free afternoons. He was irritated to find me with his friends. He often came there afterwards on his machine but we never mentioned it if we met in one of the passages, we behaved as though we knew nothing of each other outside.

Right or wrong I was so suspicious of those in the same house that I could not make friends with them and turned to the people I met at the gravel pit or who went out beagling to get away. They were what was then known as artistic and a term or two later, by permission of the authorities, we formed a Society of Arts.

Characteristically enough I was made Secretary. Too cautious to go entirely on one side or the other I listened to many a long rigmarole from the games fiends about " that awful Society of yours, I can't understand what you find in those aesthetes." It was a fearful release, I kept my feet in both camps, defended Rembrandt in the debates when they said he painted with treacle and told the house prefects the debaters were not really bad fellows. It was to lead me into extravagances of behaviour but it began as soft as any note of a distant horn.

AS we listen to what we remember, to the echoes, there is no question but the notes are muted, that those long introductions to the theme life is to be, so strident so piercing at the time are now no louder than the cry of a huntsman on the hill a mile or more away when he views the fox. We who must die soon, or so it seems to me, should chase our memories back, standing, when they are found, enough apart not to be too near what they once meant. Like the huntsman, on a hill and when he blows his horn, like him some way away from us.

As I have said it is wrong to try to recreate days that are done. All one can do is search them out and put them down as close as possible to what they now seem. A view holloa near is an agitated thing, far off it should have the charm our new sirens have when they are being tested over the next borough against the time we shall be raided. And so our memories when they are written should, like the huntsman tell that the chase is on, like the sirens that it will soon be too late and in the way that both these are at a distance they should be muted so that they shall not break on a reader's communion with

his own but only remind him by the sound so faint
of ours.

This blanketing which time or distance lends is
the more necessary when what has to be written has
no enchantment, when because it is part of the
picture so that without it only half the story could be
told there is no escape, no avoiding the recital even
if bringing back what is painful still warms a sense
of shame as though the note, so distant it may now
be no louder than a breath, will blow those embers
to a flame we have almost let die to ashes in cold
forgetfulness.

What follows must be prefaced by another death.
There were seats in our School Chapel for masters
and for the public. We had been praying at the
daily service for the recovery of one of us who was
very ill, as we had done at my first academy. When
he died, and he had not been at my house, the
school was so much bigger that most of us had not
even heard he was dead until we found we were
being asked to pray for his soul. At that moment I,
and I was not alone, looked up to where the public
were seated and saw a middle-aged couple with
tears streaming down their faces. They did not try
to mop them up and all at once we realized, how
different our reactions now, almost with a sense of
outrage that these two must be the parents. Crying
was natural at my first school, we wept at everything
but here we had a horror of tears. I remember a

girl once told me how shocked she had been to see a man blubbering at a night club. She was being unreasonable and so was I when I thought as I did then that the congregation, because we were obliged to attend, was being tricked into a display which was unfairly embarrassing or " pretty awful."

By a fine irony I was told not three days later that both my parents were dying.

It is not necessary to enter into my relations with my parents. I believe we were never far from each other's thoughts, I do not suppose a day has passed when I have not thought of them, but apart from the few inevitable frictions and those mostly came later, we were on easy terms, not too close to that intimacy which strangles or too far from intimacy of any kind.

Again, as before, when my housemaster read out the telegram he had received I felt absolutely nothing at all.

In my life I have had no similar experience. A shock blankets the mind and when I got back to my room I walked up and down a long time as I had done when I had earache at home while still at my first school. But whereas the physical pain had then made thought impossible in this case the shock made the sensation of grief, which I am not sure I have ever felt, altogether out of the question. Instead, and I fear this is horrible, I began to dramatize the shock I knew I had had into what I thought it ought to feel like.

Worse still I had known instinctively the moment my housemaster broke the news that I should so take it because after asking questions about their condition which he could not answer as the accident had been in Mexico and there were as yet no details, and after making arrangements to go up to London the next day, I made to leave but stopped at the door and said " I don't know how I shall feel about this later but I don't feel too bad now."

This was the first time I had ever said anything genuine to him and I was so ashamed after that I took good care it should be the last.

When I got back to my room I wondered how I ought to deal with anyone who came in. When someone did he managed it for me by saying " my God you do look awful," so that I was able to blurt the story out. It happened then exactly as it had at my first school with one difference, a wall was built between us by my news, his eyes grew blank and he went off at once leaving me an albino again. But where previously we had been left out because when in mourning one child was supernatural to the others now that we were older the barrier was embarrassment. We were shy of what we affected to ignore like the nasty fact of sudden death. It was not that he could be afraid I should burst out into the simple desperate crying of those parents. If I had he would have forgotten. No, what I told him separated us because it was outside his experience and so was awkward, no longer creepy but something to be dodged. It was all this for me as well, I felt even more apart than ever but I could not escape the event. It had happened to me and as I lay in bed that night I whipped myself up to more than meet it in what I more than ever felt in my self pity to be a society entirely hostile.

The next morning I had got myself into such a state that I thought everyone hated me, just when something frightful because it was so real had come about. It was still unreal and I had to remind myself over and over that it had occurred. I was helped when I picked up a morning paper, saying under my breath " well there will be no mention in this anyway," by immediately finding a short paragraph which announced there was no hope for either of my parents. Then I could blame myself for what sleep I had had and found sitting down to breakfast with fifty others a wordless inquisition on the part of each one of them although no more than five had learned my news.

The truth is I think that boys when they have shocks of this kind should be allowed to go away at once. There was nothing to be gained by not letting me take train for London until after the morning service. If I had had courage I should not have gone to morning service and so spared myself something I still do not like to remember. But I had to ask the headmaster for leave to be away over several days and the best time to do this was when he was on his way to the Chapel.

The bell was always rung once to say there was now not much more time and again to say make haste and a last bell was rung each day as those who had started late raced to get in. This left me alone in a huge space waiting for him in his purple cassock as he in his turn hurried to be last of all. I thought he was unsympathetic when he gave me leave. He was acute and if he did not say much it was probably because he saw I had worked myself up. Be that as it may it was in part the cause of what followed.

I went into the Chapel and was the last to go to my place. As I walked up the aisle I felt everyone was watching in that open curiosity of a crowd which dares to look because there are so many staring. In particular I saw that the headmaster's wife kept her eye on me. Then throughout the service I let myself go, willed myself to imagine the parents writhing in agony, pulled faces, showed all the agitation I could and at the same time, there can be no excuse, watched her to see that she got the full force of it. I think the headmaster had guessed because when I glanced at him I saw distaste on his face but she was too good to believe that anyone could be so low and was distressed.

The rest had an element of comedy. I travelled to London and went to my grandmother's house. There they had better news which left me with a great sense of anticlimax. Gerald had come up from Cambridge and was shouting with relief to one of my aunts because my father's family is always noisy when excited. My mother's family keep overquiet in a crisis and one of my mother's brothers was seated speechless behind his *Times* dressed from head to foot in black in case he had to hear the worst. Each side of the family hated the other sincerely in this situation and soon I realized there was nothing for it but to go back that same day to school. Gerald and my aunt were making plans to go out to Mexico at once and I knew they would not take me. I could have stayed with my grandmother in London but the truth is, and it was my own fault, I was at ease with none of them. I felt I had better lick my wounds back amongst the crowd I should be lost in at school for there at any rate no one would be solicitous and that, I do not know why when I blamed people for being unsympathetic, I dreaded most of all.

I had wounds to lick, not only because now that I knew my parents would get well I had time to be sorry for them but because I was horrified at myself. I could never be the same with the headmaster's wife who had always been particularly kind. I thought she must despise me beyond anyone if she knew the truth but I never could even begin to talk about it to her so as to find out where I stood. I did not like her husband because I felt he had seen through me and I could not find courage to ask him if he had. I was certain my housemaster had been very much embarrassed when he broke the news. I believed I understood his character and could not make up my mind whether he hated saying " I have bad news for you " because he disliked me or because, and it was this I feared, he dreaded I should give myself away as indeed I had. In a few weeks time I had made myself ill so that I had to be treated all because I could not talk it over with any of these people.

I was given a push further down this hill about five weeks later. When my parents were well enough to sit up in bed they had bandages swathed round their heads and necks for fun and sent photographs home as a joke. This gave me a return of hysteria. I thought it was proof of how smashed they were in spite of anything they said in their letters about how lightly they had escaped. Now at last I believe I felt genuinely sorry.

I wonder how much boys feel because they know they ought to feel ? In my case it was made harder because whatever had happened to my parents had taken place thousands of miles away where they still were, unapproachable, remote. But when very much younger, staying with cousins, the closing of a nursery door had had much the same conse-quences.

My parents used to visit Mexico every other year

and it so happened some cousins were looking after me while they were away. There was a girl of the house my age who was much bigger and as far as my memory goes, for this is a long time ago, she was managing at that time. She adopted the attitude children do when showing others on a visit the places private to themselves, their kingdom. She did not want to show me her private garden where she grew her own flowers but she had to be polite. In the result I had to see but I was not to touch. She had her spade with her which unfortunately was not of wood and this I snatched presumably to dig up her darling plot which may have held six peonies. Rightly she would have none of this and tried to stop me. She was the stronger and was succeeding when in a last attempt to get my way I swung the spade with all my strength against her leg and cut her to the bone.

My rage went out like a light switched off when I saw the blood. I screamed with remorse. We were both carried back to the house and the moment came when the nursery door was shut behind her by a grim-looking nurse. It seemed to me then a final act as though I had been cut off for ever. Then the bolt shot home and I saw nothing for it but to cut my own leg open and was carried to bed screaming for a knife. There was of course no knife, if there had been I doubt whether I should have used it. The door closing and then being barred was what seemed so fatal as later the fact of this accident to my parents having occurred in a place out of my reach set me apart, waiting for news I did not believe when it was good, in a society I felt I had estranged.

They say the fox enjoys the hunt but the sound of the horn as he breaks covert must set great loneliness on him. When he knows by the cry of the pack at his heels that the huntsman has put the hounds on then surely in so far as animals can be expected to have feelings and however cruel they may be by nature fear must enter into it, he must fear for his life.

The rabbit screams before the stoat like I shrieked for a knife in the night nursery before the stoat remorse.

Later, when the accident I have described disrupted me, I felt, and it is hard to explain, as though the feelings I thought I ought to have were hunting me. I was as much alone as any hunted fox. Only as my feelings turned and doubled in their tracks to the loud blasts of news each cable brought, as conscience the huntsman cast my feelings forward and then back until the fox I was was caught, bowled over at last into genuine surrender, there was something desperate in the noise, the howling at my heels. At this distance the noise of the pack is stilled, their music as it is called comes from over the hill, the huntsman, now an older man, blows his horn gently, and the note, now so distant it is no louder than a breath to bring forgotten embers to a glow, is shame remembered, a run across familiar country.

ONE advantage of life at school is that new friends are to hand, there are hundreds almost under the same roof and this is the reverse of London in which to be alone is to stay so, where only the threat of war will bring strangers to conversation with each other in the desert polite life carries with it, on these shifting sands which do not sing that we cling to like any cactus.

If we had gone up to a strange boy in the street to ask no more than a question we should have been politely answered but, if we were not new boys, with such a look so much as to say " you must be mad " that there was no making friends in this fashion. On the other hand there were chances in class to get to know what lay behind fresh faces, on the playing fields or, as I have described, out beagling.

There was even a school orchestra. I was one of the second violins, appropriately enough, from my first term to the last. Once a week at night we were given passes specially to go out after hours to get to practice and at the end of each term we gave a concert, reinforced by professional musicians who came down for the evening. On almost every one of these occasions my fingers sweated so much my strings broke. Rather than put on a fresh string which would have meant being continually out of tune, for I did not play well, I used to go through the motions without bringing out a sound, my bow sawing the air, my fingers following out what tune the second violins were allowed and happier at that because I played so badly. The rehearsals were amusing because we did not care how we played and the conductor was always losing his temper. But each concert, and particularly the one rehearsal with the professionals, was excruciatingly funny. Once the double bass broke a string and all the cello's took off their coats, rolled up their sleeves and set to work to fix a new one. They laughed in that bitter but uproarious way all experts have when they go to help one of themselves who has been made to look ridiculous at his job. Even the first violins were amused. Again the drummer never failed to complain he had no time to tune his drums when the key changed. I do not know enough about music to tell if this was a peculiarity of this one man's or of all drummers, but we used to look forward to it every term as well as to the fury of our conductor who never got used to him.

This and other farces gave one the chance to meet new people. The school was large and so there were boys to suit every inclination and, in the state of shock I was in, I fled the company of those in my house to a set then beginning to form. They were to be known by the term, which at school spelt leprosy, of " the aesthetes."

That is to say we hoped to arouse more than disdain, we were out to annoy by being what we called " amusing " but it is likely no notice was taken of us except by our juniors who were still in that state in which, as urchins, they welcomed anything they felt safe to mock. For ourselves we took a fearful joy in making fun of all that we thought the school held sacred. Where the majority kept in step by subscribing to a standard of worth based on proficiency at games we tried to show we were proud we were no good at football or cricket and that we despised the dull way they tried to keep in what we called their boring swim.

Our attitude was not dictated entirely by physical clumsiness although I have no doubt that any one of our number, if he had suddenly had a success at some game which counted, could have been drawn into the prefect's orbit and would soon have left us flat. But there were several of us who were without question well on for their age in literature, in their knowledge of painting and most of all in the point of view they were able to take towards the life led about us. We were witty already even by the low standard which was set by wider circles afterwards and which we were to know when we said goodbye to Oxford. Indeed one or two are no more amusing now. If we do not laugh at their jokes it is because we are too used to their attitude, precocious then but at the present time " so like old so and so."

In contrast, the masters were a poor lot and perhaps this is why our attempts to amuse seemed very funny at the time. There were no schoolmistresses of course, nothing but men. Many of these had been taken on because of their skill at games. Even those who taught modern languages with appalling accents through having made centuries for South Africa and Australia only three years before were better than the fantastic types who looked after us during the war at my first school and so they should have been, our education cost far more money now. The pity of these famous games men was that there was no subject they could teach except the game in which they specialized. They coached the school elevens, perhaps thirty boys had the benefit of their skill with a ball while no fewer than a hundred day in day out learned nothing in their classes.

One of these masters, a rowing man, once made me an ambiguous reply. I had been in his class six terms without ever having passed the time of day. I happened to come in early and thought it would be polite to say something only I could not think what. At last I went up, apologized and asked stupidly enough which was the hardest part for stroke in the Boat Race. He replied firmly " stroke always ought to have a lot in hand." This was the extent of our conversation over a period which in the end came to be two years under him and this seems absurd.

Another man, famous at a different sport, taught a language he hated and did not know. The headmaster used to come round unexpectedly to listen to his new masters so that he could find out how they handled us and on the first occasion he did this to the man I describe we witnessed an embarrassing scene. He lost his head when he saw his employer and made the mistake of trying to translate a passage himself only to come upon a word he did not know. Now I knew it and so did several others but while he in his agony was saying " this is a very difficult phrase, let me see, oh let's see," we could not prompt him however much we should have liked. He was unpopular but his torture was so great, as with some cruelty the headmaster stood waiting for him to extricate himself, that we would have helped him if it had not been tactless to show a knowledge greater than his own. We sat there sweating with him.

Another time the same master, at the outbreak of some row because he was weak and we naturally took advantage of it, threw his book down on the floor in front of his desk, buried his face in his hands and cried out very genuinely, " I can't go on." He meant in the profession he had chosen, what each one of us was paying him to do because he did not get his cheques to coach at games. For two minutes we could not be sure whether he was going to sob or be able to pull himself together. We should have seen the interest but, like the little gentlemen we were, felt nothing but horror at his having given way. Emotion was one thing that must not be shewn and here we had it naked and ashamed.

Another had thirty-six blue pencils laid out on his desk, the longest on his right and then in strict order of size they were arranged across to his left. He was a finicky man and was supposed to have counted the feathers in a tit's nest until he reached the six hundred thousandth feather when the strain became too great and he gave up after doing his eyes damage which no oculist could put right.

There were all sorts and one of them after reading through his Drill Book came out to the weekly parade of the O.T.C. under an umbrella because it was raining. We thought it triumphantly amusing at the time but now I cannot see that it was any less boring than anything we brought off. Again our company commander, a master of course, led us through a wood when we were out on manœuvres and as he began to see fields beyond the trees said, " hocus pocus here we are."

Every year, at the end of the summer term we had to go to Camp. Dressed to look like soldiers with rifles of a kind we lived for a week under canvas in great discomfort in a travesty of peace-time sol-diering, playing the amateur at a paid game which should of all others be that of life and death as much as a doctor's. In the evening like boy scouts we had sing songs in a large marquee and when volunteers were called for by the parson to tell jokes I was the only one to come forward, told two, and did not get a laugh.

In my last term at the private school we gave a sort of entertainment because one of the masters had been an actor. That is a stage was put up outside with a curtain which went down at intervals before an audience lying about like stones over a field in Ireland. For some reason there was one row of soldiers, sitting dressed in blue because they were wounded, but wild, unresponsive and remote like Irish cattle. Now some accident befell what was called the scenery so that we could not raise the curtain and I was sent in front. I asked what I should say and the master said, "Tell them anything." I talked for ten minutes before he whispered the scenery was all right again and in that time got one laugh only and that was loud and sudden from the wounded soldiers at something I had said which I had no idea was amusing. In my surprise I looked for our old tyrant and saw he was not amused.

Similarly when I foolishly accepted that general invitation which had been extended each night without response since we had been at Camp, in the middle of that strained silence my first joke left behind, I saw the prefects in my house talking to each other where they sat with a look on their faces of the most utter despair and shame. For once I had done something really frightfully awful for the school because it had made ours look awful to the boys from all the other awful schools at Camp. You may think they would have half killed me. They said they would but could do nothing because I had done no more than I had been asked.

When we had all been scouts at my first school I decided for some reason I forget that I must get out and went in tears, which was the only safe way to ask for anything there, to beg the scoutmaster to see if our old tyrant would allow me to drop out. He was one of those who when he blew his nose let off a bellow and this he now did. He then reminded me of the scout oath and said, " Once a scout a scout always Henry " and that for better or worse is what so many of us are today.

After this one experience of Camp I thought it was enough and looked into the question of resigning. I found as I had hoped that like many systems in schools such as these the Corps had been started not less than fifty years back on a voluntary basis and by searching in the library through what could be called its Charter I turned up a form of words which, if signed by one's parents, the housemaster, the Company Commander, the Colonel and the headmaster entitled one to go back to civilian life. There were advantages in this apart from escaping Camp and I

set about persuading my parents. This done I found
I had been right when I thought that if they signed
the given form of words it would be difficult for the
rest to refuse their signatures in turn and so it came
about very easily. There was no valid argument
against me, no war was threatened, we lived then in
the fool's paradise of a peace the old fools had dictated. The Colonel only remarked, as is often the
case with those in authority, conscious they are being
unnaturally reasonable, "what would happen if
everyone was like you, just tell me that." They were
not such idiots they need be told to make everything
compulsory. While they could get enough boys to
dance to their tune for what was to be found in it
they had no cause to regret my absence. Of course
I was informed that because I could now not get my
Certificate A I should have to serve as a private if we
fought a war again. As I write, by one of those
pleasant ironies which go to make life, those who
join the Territorials are being made to serve as
privates irrespective of their Certificates. They will
have to go over all that old ground again and I wish
them joy, speaking as the Auxiliary Fireman I have
now become. On the other hand if I am not killed
in the first four months the chances are I shall be
drafted into the army and by the same irony shall
likely enough be burned to death as a private. But
not because I did not go to Camp.

There were eight or nine of us who for one reason

or another had got out of the Corps. I was dining one night at the headmaster's when they were talking of how the whole contingent was to travel to London to watch the Military Tournament. I suggested that those who were left should form themselves into an ex-service man's brigade and be allowed to attend the parade in Trafalgar Square. A bishop was present and he offered to be our chaplain while the headmaster's wife said the wives of the masters should knit us a banner. So you will agree that there was nothing amusing in this although it was thought very dashing at the time and also that one was liberally treated. A Storm Trooper could never have resigned or, if he had, would never have made fun of it. I had passed before I knew out of the early Christian period of my private academy, out of the totalitarian state which is one's first year or two at a public school, into a twilight of activity in which I was not so miserable because I had found friends of my own sort.

We were allowed to form a Society of Arts.

This point is a watershed, after this there was no turning back. I determined to be a writer, the diary I began to keep with this in view was full of loud shouts about it, and a *nom de plume* was chosen, of all names Henry Michaelis. When I was photographed I wrote as follows on one of the prints:

I flatter myself that this is not in the least like me: how could it be what with the irritation at the photographer and the idiocy of being photographed. I resolutely posed myself and looked out with an easily recognizable defiance at the paste board I was to mesmerize. There is anger and resignation in that futile flabby sneer of the lips, there is a terrible lankness, toughness almost in the figure. Altogether a horrible photograph.

Five years later I had got far enough on to write this:

BARQUE

I sail on the sea by wind which is in the sky and I am the most beautiful thing on the sea. Stiffly I go, am borne upon the waters, and when I am near land the white gulls wheel then settle in the plenty of my rigging.

When I am near land on that land the people will come out from houses and the airman look down from sky at my white sails on the silver sea. Or, through the great waste, swiftly softly straining, the birds will turn to me also then or, when are no more birds, then also I am most beautiful thing that is on the sea, alone, alone, my sails leaping full with the wind which is in sky I go stiffly, I am most beautiful of all.

Again and this time less literary:

They have gone to bed too early, there is no courtesy now in guests. For as the woman may lie awake after the man has finished, so may we be sent to our rooms by the empty chairs. Surely mind, animated by the unaccustomed flow of talk, may also have its consummation. Then when we feel there is no more to be said, then we may go and lie on our beds at ease. We have functioned. But tonight and on such nights as these, I am an unsatisfied lover.

These three pieces I have quoted are the expression of moods and what interest they may have lies not so much in what they describe as in how they are written. Thus the set exercise given second shows command of words in the way these are quite successfully repeated but between the first and the third, which are both yells about self, there is a whole expanse of wounds beginning to be scabbed, raw in the first piece healing in the last and in what I write now on the same subject grown over I hope by an attitude on which the success or failure of this part of my book must depend. For death in my case I am afraid will come too soon, before this attitude is established and the end of my time at school and the two years at Oxford sufficiently digested to regurgitate as doves in spring to other doves whose interest they wish to rouse.

What difference there may be, and it is obvious to me at least, between the first and third of these pieces is due to the five years which lie between. There is already in the amount by which the style has varied a sense of the remote. The extent to which that remoteness has been settled in what I am writing here is the ten years lived since the third piece was put down hastened by that threat of war which drives one into a last attempt to explain objectively and well.

One comes with the first real friends made to begin to think of oneself mostly in relation to others. Thus before I had had a real exchange with anyone I was writing on the back of a photograph what I thought of my face. Five years later I had the sense to bring others in when I wrote about myself in order to blame as much as possible on others. There is no excuse for sneering at the flabby lips but the reader can have less cause to complain about the desertion of having to go up alone to bed. Everyone has had that experience when they have been in love as I was then. I was equally self-absorbed when both pieces were written but the last is the better done. My task is to show how this came about, how the style, which changed as a girl's complexion changes with the hours she keeps, emerged into 1928, the date beyond which I do not hope to go; how this self-expression grew and how it altered.

Any account of adolescence is necessarily a study of the fatuous and yet it would be wrong to treat it on the lines of comedy as could so easily be done. It seems to me that everyone under the age of forty and in some cases many for the rest of their lives are influenced by what they went through at school and this was of course largely made up of the growing pains they suffered or enjoyed. Those who did too well there may not have come to much in after life because the effort they made then was too great; there are men who have won every prize and burned themselves out and who go about now amiable but defeated. For every one of these there are a hundred whose mistake it was to do too well at games so that they were too happy to do more than relive their successes over again once they had left. The trouble with the clubmen where I came from was that they were so excessively pompous.

We took ourselves seriously but we did not stalk heavily about as did the members of the prefects' club. This may be because we were not allowed to have airs and it is true that a year or two later there was some question that one of us might be elected and in that case, as I have said before, not only would he have had nothing more to do with our Society, but he would have been as pompous as the rest no doubt.

Our leading spirit, an extraordinarily able and amusing man for his age, thought in his last year that he would give the prefects' club an oyster tea. Now when the Society of Arts was formed I had been made secretary appropriately enough, that is, the kind of executive who does what the others tell him and has no importance. I was too sly by far to put my eggs in one basket and managed to keep in with the prefects in my house as well. One of the two leaders we had had at the time when I knew no one outside was now not only a prefect himself but in the prefects' club at last. It was my job to find out whether the club would come to the tea. It was understood no one else was to be invited. After talking this over they let it be known they would attend if asked and so my friend ordered a room and sent for his barrel. I had been invited also but at this moment, and it is characteristic, I did not dare. Instead I arranged an appointment in London with the dentist. I was afraid if the party were a failure, and actually it was a great success, that I should not be able to stand quite where I had. But I cannot say where my friend stood after he brought it off or whether he had any chance to be elected. He never did get in. All I know is that when we went up to Oxford he made friends with all the exclubmen from our school who were most worth knowing. He was for ever in and out of their rooms and in those days I saw little more of him.

When at last in my turn I was a prefect I was told by one of the clubmen in my house that he had put me up for election. This he had done not because he thought I should get in, I was unknown to more than four or five by sight and to none of them by reputation, but for the reason, touching enough, that it would be a good thing for the house to have another clubman in it. After I had failed by the greatest possible number of black balls he was able to propose, when next his turn came, the friend he had in mind outside.

What never lost interest was the behaviour of those who thought they had a chance during the weeks before an election. This is not to say that, if I had been in the running, I should not have been as absurd, but it is a great consolation to watch the failure of some who pretend to great things, their confidence and then the angry bewilderment with which the news leaves them. It was one of the merits of our life at school that any reverse of such a kind had to be taken quietly, not of course from any other reason than that if it were not so accepted they would never have the chance again and one of the demerits that those who were chosen almost always took their election with a humility they lost too soon and so showed how false this was. In fact I maintain that, of the two, ours was a more genuine standard.

Once they had been elected they were allowed to walk arm in arm with each other and, when they met a friend who was not in the club, they could arm him as well. No one else could do this, it was a privilege, and so our old tyrant's ruling was reversed when he had said at my first school " if I find any more of you little beasts walking arm in arm I shall make him wear petticoats." But what was interesting was to watch and see whether they would go on arming friends from whom they had been inseparable and who were now divided more sharply than is possible in after life by the success, the canonization election meant. Royal children go to public schools and while there are treated as far as possible like anyone else. When they go down their being royal catches them up and they cannot be as others are. When boys were elected to the prefects' club they became royal, they could not be like the ordinary prefects and some of them have stayed uncommon clubmen all their lives.

Our trouble was that it was not easy to get people to join our club, those on the fringe were not keen to be demonstrably mixed up with the " awful " lot we were still supposed to be. The fact that we were allowed to have meetings and that the headmaster had once attended one of our debates made sensibly enough no real difference to the distaste with which we were regarded. It may have saved us from persecution by those who were trying to get on and to distinguish themselves, who watched for a chance to do the popular thing, but our having been recognized by the authorities did not encourage the bashful to let it be known they were with us. Public opinion at school is as powerful as it is because by far the greater number want the same kind of success. They find anyone who does not share this intolerable for the reason that he casts a reflection on the amount of effort they have to expend to have a chance to succeed. We found anyone who felt he could not afford to join us as much a traitor as any blackleg in a strike but at the same time we had hopes for several terms we might be able to interest the prefects' club and even, but this was a wild dream, to have perhaps one of our number elected by a sort of wild surprise.

I suspect this was why my friend invited them all to the oyster tea and if they did not elect him at least they all went. We did not know it then but we were carrying out exactly what goes on in London. Almost every artist is a snob and will move heaven and earth to have a smart party. Money did not come into it at school, at Oxford money was everything, in London it is not all money but part of our plan with this society of arts was to get ourselves in by the back door in the end.

We met in the Art schools under the presidency of the Arts Master. One of us read a paper after which there was supposed to be a debate. In no case did anyone answer a point made, it was like a conversation between women, whoever got up to speak only did so to show off.

It was a long low room with skylights and on shelves along the walls earth-red pots, unglazed jars which generations had had to draw and white casts rubbing noses when the clock struck, now dead and still. It was always dusk in there but it had charm because there was no other dirty room in the whole school. Wherever a shelf ended watercolours were hung up of the same casts and pots standing next to them and however badly these were drawn the repetition on paper and in colour of so much that was before the eye made the place amicably unreal like a living joke.

Here with a great sense of settling everything, we

said, one after the other, that art was not representation. Here, under the yawns of the Arts Master who it so happened was a charming man known throughout Europe for his skill at a game, we had what came as close to those talks which are supposed to be exchanged by undergraduates in which the course of life is plotted so they say like bringing a smack into Southampton, talks which I have never heard and which I do not believe come to a stop when I come in.

We can never be sure how much of everything we miss by being unsympathetic but it is always possible this may amount to very little. It would be wearisome to put down what I heard at our meetings or at the rehearsals and performances of the puppet shows we gave later. All I know is it gave me confidence even if there was nothing in it so that, like everyone else, I began to write a novel.

I began to meet girls.

WHEN I went home for the holidays there were two sisters who lived near, one dark and the other fair, one married and the other who lived in the same house, a widow. Both were young, great friends and beautiful.

They were fond of entertaining, had house-parties at weekends and asked those who lived close over to play tennis every Saturday and Sunday they were not staying away themselves.

The court was out at the back by stables which were built round three yards, brick buildings over cobblestones the colour in sunlight of dried seaweed on white marble with the smell so like but not the same as when under a hot sun the small wind blows inland the bite of sea on a temple grown over and uncovered at low tide.

Out of sight the players called " mine." Shutting the eyes in this glare it was easy to believe they were away over a sand dune as I stood in the slight suspense that leaving the party covered me as the turn of the tide will hang over the waves breaking.

In such brightness the dazzled eyes looked inside these buildings half expecting to find upended rowing boats or, propped up with timber, for these were large stables, sailing boats with deep keels. It came as a surprise to find a horse standing with its coat part of that resonant glow of shade which, with the tang of soiled straw, might have been at the opening of a cave down on the sands where they are carting seaweed the sun has dried.

For every now and then I had to go away out of nervousness. While I could usually make the women laugh the older men they had down to stay and who were always about made me nervous because I had nothing in common with the attitude they adopted. They appeared to be on too good terms with themselves, always doing what they liked, living like irresponsible kings. I know now that one or two were racked with worries and they may have longed to be back, even on my terms, at school again but looking at them as I did through the eyes of my sixteen winters, at the harvest festival of their thirties, they seemed unapproachably free and, once the women's backs were turned, so learnedly coarse.

Everyone's view of people is coloured by their circumstances and my life up to this time made me see these two women in a light altogether remote from any that shines on this world. The dark one had vast dark eyes with a kind of way she used to look at you as though you were standing blinded in the sun while she had caught you trying to look in where she was in that echoing shade, as though she had all that glare which was about you inside her and knew it well, inviting you even to match yours with her, mocking you for staying out while absolutely refusing to let you come inside. She had a barbaric extravagance in her eyes, in that look she could turn on at will and which so confused me that I could never agree the rest of her with this power she had when I was under her sight. It was an unalterable mystery that she could look so different to what I thought she was, that when poetry yelled out of her magnificent eyes she could laugh at such men's jokes, that she could laugh at all even at mine when just to see her and the rings on her fingers made me wonder did she take these off when she washed her white hands that were so much a part of her sapphires.

The other was lovely rather than beautiful with a wonderful laugh. She had no interest of any kind so far as I could tell in anything except hunting and yet when we sat down to a meal, and they always put us next each other, we would laugh so much at the things we invented that the dark one, abandoning her neighbours, would call down the long table to ask what it was all about.

I was entirely uncertain of my position in this house I so loved and was overcautious for I do not suppose they ever thought of me again until they had got another party together. On their side I expected them to think me rather mad and, in return for the pains I took, to let me be in the breathless jokes we had, in the sort of privacy I thought we had built round us.

They were keen on amateur acting and were for ever getting up performances in the village hall in aid of something or other. They had asked me before to take a part and I had refused, my first school and then camp had put an end to that. Now on an evening when I had stayed to dinner my dark friend said in front of a large party she wished I would act with them. I said I could not really. Then turning on that remembered look which was so much of all I could call to mind of what I had ever read, she said, " Henry, if you do I shall let you kiss me." I blushed and, it was rare enough, could find nothing to say, to express how false I thought she had been to let me in for this in front of all these people and yet how extraordinarily generous it was of her to offer to let me put my mouth on what I then felt to be all the race of women laughing.

I did not act in her play and so she did not kiss me.

It may have been some time later that we gave a dance at home and of course these two women came over for it. Now I had refused to learn to dance, stupidly enough holding at that period that it was a low way to get on with anyone. My father took the same view but now, each of us older by twenty years, we both dance whenever we get the chance. Accordingly we decided to slip away early, lock ourselves into the billiards room and have a game.

We were both mad on billiards and played every day for hours. Nobody was allowed to play fives on the table and while we were at it anyone who, in spite of our frowns, came in and sat on the sort of dais there was at one end had to keep entirely quiet and still. In this we were right because much of the charm lies in the green cloth under electric lamps with the three balls, two white, one red, going through movements geometrically exact in a hush while the slow score is chanted. A drop cannon which gathers them by the top cushion is a stroke so precise in the way the three widely separated balls are brought together within the span of the fingers of one hand, so leisurely but so inevitable when played right that silence is the tribute the ordered evolutions each must roll softly through, is the tribute this shot demands.

We played well and when the game was over we locked the room so that no guests could get in to begin fooling with the table and went to bed up the back stairs, the music coming to us as a faint accompaniment to the drum. My room was some way off in this big house and as I undressed I could hear no sound of the dancing until I opened the window to listen for it in that reluctance to admit one is wrong to refuse enjoyment which leads to self pity and regret. I thought they were idiots that they could amuse themselves to a band's music but I wished I had been the best dancer in the room. I turned the light out, got into bed and prepared to have no rest, pitying myself for being forgotten when a woman said " Henry, Henry," outside the door. My heart choked me. She came in darker and more beautiful than ever and I was dazzled again when she put on the light. She had brought a young man who was bored and embarrassed. She said I must dress and come down at once, she gave no reason, it was enough for her that she had expressed the wish by making a statement. She then began to examine the furniture and everything standing on it with that malice women have about bedrooms. I refused, I said I could not get up now and, bored suddenly or for some reason or other, she said as she turned to go that if I was not down before the end of the next dance she would come to fetch me. She had not looked at me yet and, as she was going out, greatly daring I called after her " if you come to pull me out of bed I'll take my pyjamas off now in case you do." She immediately turned her look on, and while her young man was dying of it she said she would be back to see I did nothing so silly. With that she went and I did not take off my pyjamas.

At the same time I did not get out of bed and lay there wondering whether she would come back as she had said.

After some time she did return, this time with her

174

sister and two more men who talked to each other as though I were not in sight. I lay in great excitement as if these girls were going to carry out an operation on me. They came up to the bed and the dark one said rather crossly, " Why didn't you get up and dress when I told you," and the other, before I could reply, said " What's this I hear about your taking your pyjamas off." The first went on, and I still had said nothing, " Oh Henry you haven't really, have you ? " in a disinterested voice and then I think because they knew their dancing partners were there they lost what little interest they had and again began to look about the room. I felt very foolish and said, " Well, if you go out I'll dress and come down," and they said " that's right " and " what an extraordinary room you have," stayed on for a moment and then left both saying " and hurry up " over their shoulders. All this time they had not said a word to the men, one of whom, as he went out last, gave half a smile in my direction to be polite.

There was nothing odd about my room ; I have always kept any I have had bare of possessions. There were no photographs because the Society of Arts held that photographs were abominations, there were no extravagant hair brushes or anything to give any line on what I was like. Why they chose to come up I do not know, possibly it was no more than friendliness, a quality I have never been able to recognize, and why this visit in the night has given me to think of it over and over again I cannot tell. I do not know why they came up from crowds of couples to a boy, out of the hot circling room of people, out of bare shoulders, jewellery, heads helmeted like theirs with every kind and colour of soft hair but as a result I felt I had grown up and did not presume on the incident because I had the sense to realize they were not for me, that these two older women would tolerate me only if I did not try to bother them on their preserves one of which obviously a dance must be.

The next term, the first of my last year, I went back to school quite an old gentleman not only because of the experience just told but also by the circumstance that nearly all my friends had gone up to Oxford. I was left almost last of the original members of the Society of Arts and could find so few to carry on with the debates that these were allowed to drop.

I played football for the house but did not get my colours and was given a new room, much larger only it opened on to the stairs. I was querulous about the noise people made going down them, an attitude which agreed with the part I played now, that of the survivor of a golden age who was already beginning to take his place with women, one who was older than his contemporaries.

Two friends and I used to go out on Sunday afternoons to a public house where we drank sherry, never more than two or three glasses. Then it was time to hurry back to evening service and we ran in the tophats we were made to wear that day back along lanes thinking that within a year we should never have to run home from pubs again. We imagined we were drunk. Standing in the tides of the organ and all the voices as everyone joined in to sing the last hymn we thought we swayed with drink and catching each other's eye laughed from the happiness of something daring shared, that secret of being fast which made it all worth while.

Hurrying back from one of these expeditions we came on a boy we knew letting himself out of a surburban villa in which I was told he was supposed to have a mistress. That was the only time I heard anything of that nature at school. Perhaps it was because I was not the sort of person to whom people describe that kind of experience, possibly that is still true to this day, but I heard of no one's triumphs with girls and suspect that, as yet, these were rare enough.

Once, a year later, when I had left and my parents had sent me to France to polish up my French before going to Oxford, I was walking back to the flat in which I was a paying guest as quickly as I could because I was late for lunch. As I came to the last turning before the street this flat was in there was a girl making her way along and the moment I set eyes on her back as I was catching her up she put on speed and I knew she thought I was following her. She did not turn round but the look of her back and bottom was agitated. A year or so before this I would have dropped behind, I had a horror of embarrassing people or of being what I called tiresome by catching women's eyes in the street so that mine would be fixed on the pavements with a look of absurd denial such as is not often found even in young priests. But I thought I was old enough now to go on with my haste to be in time for lunch when I saw she had turned into my street. At this point I all but gave her a minute to get well ahead and if it had not been a crime in this household to be late for meals I might have slackened pace although I saw that it would be terrible if she were to go into my building. This is what she now did, almost running by this time. To open the door of a French block of flats it was necessary to push a button which rang a buzzer in the porter's lodge and this delayed her until, as the porter pressed his button which released the door and she rushed inside to shut the gates of the lift on herself and I, who was at her heels, fled in an agony of embarrassment past the lift up the dark stairs muttering " pardon, pardon," I was out of breath at the horror of what I thought I must have put into her mind. So horror-struck that when she had pulled herself together and sent the lift up to the floor she wanted, I, who by that time had run almost up three stories, cowered in the darkest corner as the lift went grinding past with inside it that light from the one lamp under which I was afraid she stormed and raged. I do not suppose now she was at all angry.

In the flat next door were two sisters, the daughters of a doctor. Morning and evening as I sat in my room behind lace curtains trying to get on with the novel they came out on the balcony and apostrophized the pigeons in those long drawling tones the French use when they mean to impress with something outside the logic of their thoughts. Being as I was I did not try to get to know them. Undoubtedly they had heard from our servant telling theirs in the endless spying which goes on in such circles exactly the time I tried to work each day because they were regular with this performance which was never, to the delight of the bachelor with whom I was staying, given during the hours when I was expected to visit museums and churches.

While I was in Paris my parents gave me an allowance. Wisely indeed this was small but with care not to spend unnecessarily enough was left each month for a night in the dance halls of the Rue Fontaine. It was a far cry to be in that street when the American fleet was in and yet not so far. The most I ever saw was one woman empty her glass in a man's face and how tame this was to what I had imagined in the cell my room had been, overlooked by the School Chapel. One woman smacked

another on her behind and the slap rang out with
the ring of flesh slapped because she wore nothing
under her skirt so that I was reminded my mother
had told me how little all girls wore under their
evening dresses. When I got drunk as I did then for
the first time and, insatiable for conversation, found
how good a talker the French tart is, I compared it
with all I had known to be amazed at how little
different the street could be.

The places I describe were not brothels. The girls
could be taken home but there was nothing for that
purpose on the premises. There was usually a band
I should know now to be bad, a large bar, not much
room for dancing and then a number of tables at
which it was obligatory to pay for champagne. I
used to go with an older man I had made friends
with at the British Embassy. He did not have much
more money than myself and we had an understanding that on no account were we to be separated.
Whether it was because of my age I do not know but
it had the result that we behaved carefully and well.
Everyone else did the same.

In those days large numbers of Greeks, Rumani-
ans, Argentines and Cubans attended, it was as
natural for them to go as to take a walk after church.
They spent a great deal of money. My friend and I
sat at the bar drinking champagne cocktails which
were the cheapest long drinks to be had. Our
trouble was to drink steadily and yet have enough

money to last till dawn. The girls sat by on high stools keeping an eye on those dark men at the tables and for some hours it would be impossible to get connected talk with them, they were always being taken away to dance. Then by the time things were sorted out about four in the morning you could settle down with one who had failed to get off and indulge in a long two hours' conversation which, in my case, was the first complete exchange of views with nothing kept back I had ever had.

I talked admirably, knew the language well, and could make them talk up. Although I can remember hardly anything of what passed it was the first time I had experienced the release, the sense of constipation eased, which at that age frankness with a girl in no more than words can bring and this feeling next morning, with the guilt of clothes covered with scent is a thing most people carry with them to the end of their lives.

Going to what we now know as a night club in London with a friend is a serious thing. The band should be coloured, the room dark, we should be tired and not so sober as to be afraid to tell the truth but not so drunk as to be incapable of lying. For dance music well played has come to be a sort of blood transfusion I need at least once a week. More than that, since interest in what goes on about us has been sharpened by the fear of death and we have been left less sure than ever of anything except

the extraordinary behaviour of acquaintances and
friends, discussing these is the exchange we can have
in the kind of forcing house a night club will always
be, and the indiscretions, the lies which give the
underlying truth away, all this so far as I can tell is
what goes to make up the bargain basement of the
store our lives now are, in the receiver's hands. That
is we are not to be bought and sold but as I see it
people are taking a last look round. Picking,
fingering, saying good-bye to what they could use
to drape their hearts where everyone now wears his
in the stress of the times, on his sleeve, not naked as
hearts will be when the war comes, still covered but
in a kind of strip-tease with rapidly changing, always
fewer and ever more diaphanous clothes; in this
way, in such places anyone can divest himself of one
more protective covering and in exchange turn over
another's discarded skin cast between his hands.

In Paris of the time I write the sense of pleasure I
retained was largely of guilt and the release I got had
a great deal to do with the feeling it was wrong to
talk with tarts.

The history of this phase is not one of situations, it
is one of talks. In the last three terms at school those
of us who were ambitious had long conversations
about all we hoped to do when we went out into the
wide world. In Paris with " hostesses " I believe they
were entirely about the difference between men and
women, not in the sense our old tyrant meant at my

first school but as regards the way I saw things, that is myself, in relation to life, that is the girl whoever it might be who, hired with drinks, would discuss this intelligently and with knowledge if nothing better offered. In the South of France where I was sent to finish off, at a big country house and a large family with everyone speaking from noon to midnight, the women talked life and the men politics. They were too circumspect to bring their own experience into play. They were so objective they might have been telling a news film which had been of interest only for the dry fun they had had out of it. They were brilliant and detached as chandeliers at a party. In all this there was more to admire but less for me to find. But at Oxford some four or five months later the dons I got to know would have no discussion on the difference between women and men, or of politics or life without personalities. Here, too cocksure, we argued from the particular to the general and, for the first time, always with that spice of personal malice which was to persist and without which any long conversation was afterwards to seem unnecessarily general. Here therefore situations began to take first place in any discussion. It was usually some excess which had driven a man into an absurd corner we could describe and laugh about and twist to make a mirror of the world outside we did not know. But in London, with the advent of love making people spin like tops completely out of control, we blossomed onto a circus world that could only rationally be discussed half drunk to a nigger band playing swing in a darkened place, for only then does everything seem possible.

There were situations in the South of France. There was a girl who when she arrived was in one of these herself. As she got out of the car she put her arms round an older woman and chanted, " Ah, madame, the miseries of life." This made me intensely nervous, it was the sort of direct statement not often made before strangers in England. Her mother had died, her father was not behaving well, and she was half frantic because she was badly off and yet could not stay at home. She was thin and dark, pale with big foreign eyes and I was soon writing poetry to her. This they found natural, it was the possible outcome that alarmed them. I read these poems aloud to everyone so that for three days they dropped politics, forgot to mention their sort of life and for twelve hours each day discussed with detachment the eternal folly of mixed marriages. We spent the whole time in the one big room. Occasionally a man would get up and go out, never a woman, but he would be back within fifteen minutes with a fresh argument on the topic they were handling.

I was out of my room by ten each morning and every now and again I would see this girl who was often down before the others. We had long talks the

subject of which was prearranged. We settled, and
it was my suggestion, that, as we were to be here six
weeks together, we should talk for a fortnight as
though we were engaged, for another two weeks as
though we had just been married, and for the time
that was left as though we had been married for
ages. The French like to have everything clearcut,
she would have nothing more than this as she made
plain at once, and she was brilliant at it. That is
why she could not reproach me for the poems,
logically they were a part of our game and the fact
that they were read aloud argued I was not entangled.
I had not yet met with the character who blames one
for it all, that one should fall in love with her, that
one should be so foolish as to write her poetry and
then that one should have the impudence to read it
out. They were cleverer, they only thought it would
be silly to get married. But she was cleverest.

We all played bridge. They never bid clubs and
only led them with reluctance.

This house was on top of a hill and in the garden
where no flowers grew there were seats from which
you could look twenty miles up a valley to the
Pyrenees. After the heat of the day they all of
them sometimes wandered out to carry on with
a discussion from this spot, each one making formal
acknowledgment of the view before he in his turn
developed the argument. The one thing they would
stop for was a buzzard that stole chicks from the

farmyard where in long stalls the white velvet oxen lay in glowing shade the colour of their loving eyes. The buzzard was announced by its shadow for the sky would still be too bright to search and then we would all shriek without moving from the seats. Noise would not alter its course. In three minutes the shadow would come travelling back and in a moment be gone and they would go on with the discussion where they had left it. Each made formal acknowledgment of the loss our host had endured while they took up the argument in just the way that bird had stooped at the running chick, like any point of view each in his turn advanced for the next to swoop on. Their conversation was one raid after another superbly done, not into enemy country because they were charming people but rather from the natural activity of their minds, as birds after food. When I had finished two months there I spoke French perfectly.

It was harvest time. The heat was astounding. The sun left no colour in anything and it was only when the eyes had rested in shade for some moments that the oxen could be seen in their stalls and after another moment that their eyes could be distinguished fixed on one's own in staring unspeakable silence as if stricken down by love and yet horrorstruck. I tried to write in the afternoons and opened the shutters while the house cracked with the heat, every beam, every piece of the parquet floor staccato. Below was a tangle of undergrowth and ivy throttled trees, the ground, as one had been warned, infested by snakes for a spring came up in the middle of it, thus making possible the heightened growth. There hung over all the incessant rattling of cicadas and every now and again there was a simultaneous shot and thud shot thud as our host, an Olympic champion, fired his revolver at cracks in this castle with yard-thick walls. The cicadas would stop for a moment and then go on but the sun, the trap drummer, beat all day pounding the blood through one's ears. And always if one listened the drone of conversation rising every so often to shrill cries as one or the other swooped upon a point.

It was all so dry and yet the low hill opposite shimmered as though glass lay across the window with water pouring down it, oh God the afternoons there they were a time for screaming.

From one o'clock till three I would labour at the book and by that time had written the following, an improvement on what had been put on the back of the photograph two years before and on the whole not a bad piece of writing:

He was alone for the moment. Nan had left him to take a cup of tea. The nurse was taking the daily walk that was necessary to her trade union health, and Mrs. Haye had gone up to the village to console Mrs. Trench, whose week-old baby was dying. Herbert,

leaning on the sill of the kitchen window, was making
noises at Mrs. Lane while she toyed with a chopper,
just out of his reach. Weston was lost in wonder, love
and praise before the artichokes, he had a camera in
his pocket and had taken a record of their splendour.
Twenty years on and he would be showing it to his
grandchildren, to prove how things did grow in the
old days. Twenty years ago Pinch had seen better.
Harry was hissing over a sporting paper; Doris in an
attic was letting down her hair, she was about to plait
the two soft pigtails. Jenny, the laundry cat, was very
near the sparrow now, by the bramble in the left-hand
corner of the drying-ground.

On the other hand at the same period I could write
as badly as in the following:

The air began to get rid of the heaviness, and so
became fresher as the dew soaked the grass. A black-
bird thought aloud of bed, and was followed by another
and yet another. The sun was flooding the sky in
waves of colour while he grew redder and redder in
the west, the trees were a red gold too where he
caught them. The sky was enjoying herself after the
boredom of being blue all day. She was putting on and
rejecting yellow for gold, gold for red, then red for
deeper reds, while the blue that lay overhead was
green.

THE war, as is known, led to inequalities in the standard of living. In every class there were some who came out with a better position than they had had before, and some who were not so well off. High wages had been earned by the great majority who had stayed at home while many had come back after risking their lives to be offered a small return for the services they had rendered. The industries of this country were obliged to change over from the production of goods needed in time of war to those used in commerce in times of peace. Those who had stayed at home to make munitions could no longer earn the wages they had been paid when labour was short and time rather than money was the first consideration; those men who, on their return from overseas, had been offered " a land fit for heroes to live in " as likely as not had found unemployment waiting in the homes they might never have seen again.

There are not two or three social classes but hundreds well defined throughout Britain and not one of these escaped the effects of war. Those who had made large savings out of armaments in most cases lost them in the readjustment which came to a head in the slump of 1923. The wage earner was lucky at that time to be in work. The men and women who lived off fixed interest bearing securities found they could buy less. Everyone was affected but, as always, those who had least felt it most.

This was a time of great difficulty we were fortunate to get through without some kind of upheaval. We had had four years of a life and death struggle when every argument able propagandists could put forward to spur the people on to win had been rammed down each individual throat by the loss of life; there could have been no family which could not point to the death in battle of one near to it. The phrase then was " we gave our sons." " For what ? " was the cry in 1923. It will be the same this time.

The countries which had been defeated cracked first. Everyone knows what happened in Russia and in those days there were few who remained indifferent, they either admired Lenin or distrusted his views. There was less apathy then than now and it would have been difficult to find many content to regard that revolution as an interesting experiment. It seemed likely Germany would follow suit, a country too close to our own for its system of government to be of indifference to us. Indeed, as hardly anyone in England had read Marx before Lenin preached, most of what we heard of Russia was entirely new and therefore the more arresting.

All this is common ground and none of my business. But it had its effect on my contemporaries and is of interest for that reason. If, owing to the lucky chance that we lived in luxury we did not experience hardship and that, being so young we had not had to risk our lives only to find insecurity at last, even if we did not eat one bun less each day because of it all we heard about it, were uneasy and wondered whether our parents would be allowed to keep their money and whether we really ought to inherit when they died.

Much of a public school training is aimed at the conscience of the individual: the " do you think you are doing your best for the school ? " And conscience where having money is concerned, while easily forgotten once one has begun to enjoy its fruits or crab. apples is worrying all the time one is waiting for a real allowance, sufficient that is for someone, who has been to that sort of public school, to keep up appearances in London! For we were now, upon going up to Oxford, either to become money snobs or too sensitive to the difference money makes. At my public school I had hated every other face for fear the owner was a lord, at the university I was to court the rich while doubting whether there should be great inequalities between incomes. I had a sense of guilt whenever I spoke to someone who did manual work. As was said in those days I had a complex and in the end it drove me to go to work in a factory with my wet podgy hands.

In my last term at school I went up to Oxford for a week-end to be interviewed by the authorities at the college I was to join. The friends who had already left school took me down at night to a club which had its rooms in the slums of the town. The reason why it was out of the way in one of those back streets must have been that the members made so much noise. It was a drinking club but was more, in the terrific roar of its evenings, the quarrels the shouting and extravagance it was a sign of the times.

As a rule men stay at the University for about three years so that the period of which I write was soon after the fabulous generation had gone down who fought in the war and, when they were demobilized, went up to Oxford to become undergraduates. They had left their mark, that is the authorities had become used to riotous behaviour and had not objected because these men had not been boys who had just left school. We who had done no more than this were influenced by all that had gone on in England during the war, especially by the difference in the standards, if not in the observance, of morals. So that in my own case I had a feeling it is hard to explain almost as though I had missed something through being too young to fight, that I had not come home on leave from the front. I felt I had to make up for lost time which I had not had time to lose. But possibly it was due in part to the fact that my friends were older by having gone up to Oxford

so that it was not so much my wanting to catch up
with the war and the time immediately after as it
was that I should catch up with my friends who, as
I knew from their letters and as I was soon to learn
from experience, had had a long start. It made no
difference that this should only be a matter of six
months for they had become another generation.

I was led up some dark stairs into a low room
crammed with people shouting with laughter and
was at once made to shake hands with a waiter who
had difficulty in putting down the tray to take my
hands in his. He was dead drunk. The waiters were
encouraged to drink and most of them had to be sent
off to homes, they never lasted long. There was a
man with what I took to be a painted face standing
singing on a grand piano wearing a cloak. Someone
gave me a German mug full of what from the mug I
took to be beer but when I tasted it, found to be
very much stronger. In a moment the noise, the
heat, the smoke, the crowd and not so much the
drink made me tipsy. And I cannot describe the
place any further because on all the occasions I went
there afterwards I never was sober once. If it lives in
the memory it is as a mirage of " good " times and
those times. I had come from a place where one was
not allowed to smoke to another where this was the
least one could do and where the tutors, as I was to
find, did not even allow one to call them " sir." Is
it any wonder that I went back to my last few weeks

at school impatient for these to be over ? So that it
came as a surprise to catch a lump in the throat
when, as I went at the end to get my leaving book
from the headmaster, expecting to be told I had
wasted my time, he said no more but as much as
" we shall miss you." Thinking it over afterwards
I made sure he said this to everyone, the phrase was
so obviously tactful but parting from anything, even
a distasteful experience, is enough at any age to make
anyone doubt themselves. I know a girl who cries in
the taxi going home after a week-end party she has
hated the whole time and she cries only because she
is leaving and there are others, some of them men,
who will never say good-bye. This at my school it
was impossible not to do. As the church has its say
in birth, at marriage and in death so here there was a
rigmarole which surprised one into minding as when
on the news films one sees any scene of parting
between strangers and however much one may not
want to, is caught into an inevitable experience. All
the same I was glad to go.

When I said good-bye in the South of France they
all gathered round and told the journey's fortune in
cards, arguing over the way one card turned or fell
next to the other with as much passion as they ever
used towards their politicians. They foretold a railway accident I should be in on the way home. It
came to pass but shall find no place here, it was no
different from what might have been expected, and

was an uninteresting trick to have been played. I did
not like to leave France.

It must be the greatest lump of all in dying if our
condition is that we are conscious of it at the time.
Regret, remorse, the broken bottles our lives are.
The French, so practical, cry readily at parting, the
Russians, and we were reading Tchekov then, have a
minute's silence before the journey. It may be they
have this custom because when they travel they have
so far to go but when the time comes there cannot be a
distance greater than death takes us nor, as I had
come to think, one so final. Every farewell, as the
French have it, is to die a little. Calling these to
mind now may be in a way to die a little less.

It is impossible when saying good-bye to be certain
that where one is going will be any better than what
is being left. It is so much on the cards it may be
worse. At this school the most successful of those
leaving sang a leaving-song at their last school concert, a sentimental jingle promising never to forget.
Having had so few good-byes I was surprised that I
should mind so much and went to Oxford feeling as
though I were arriving for the first time at my first
school, uneasy, afraid because my friends were
marked men, they were æsthetes still, sorry I was
what I am.

In Oxford bells ring all day from clocks and
churches, they strike the hours with long tunes even
the quarters take some time and in the day it is

impossible to go through the town without hearing a single bell somewhere tolling. At home there was a sweet tumbling music morning and evening on Sundays but here every creed had its church or chapel and each of these its loud-voiced clock which chimed so that there was an unceasing appeal to one's intelligence which only stopped at night, continual good-byes. At first this ringing ringing charmed the senses. There is only one town I know where there are no bells or tunes at the quarter-hour and that is Moscow. It is a pity to have none and better to have too few. For the stone the colleges are built with flakes away in course of time. On the older Oxford buildings you might think the wet of shower and rain had grown a stone fungus over those fronts of ancient gaiety. In this way the bells, so overdone they soon lost their charm, by never leaving one alone seemed, as the sea eats out a temple to cover it with weed, to have bitten into the black porticos and walls their sound was forever lapping.

Every day one died a little. The difference now was that one knew it.

The room I was given overlooked a lawn scythed or mown five hundred years in the centre of some cloisters. Outside the window a riddled gargoyle looked down and stuck his crumbling tails in an eternal gesture at my fireplace. The cloisters were paved with stone and echoed as well as increased the sound so that you could hear each step and every word of those who went walking talking through them as they did all day and half the night. It is all so old and the noise of the bells, high and low, is old, the same in centuries. Men of the same age, equally young, have lived there over and over for as many years. Because of all this and partly because I had begun to drink heavily I thought I should go crazy.

For one term only I was, as a friend said, "the most popular man of his year" and dined out every night. Mine was the sort of welcome a man gets who is well liked but who has come late, for a time he is made much of, they say "how splendid you managed to get here" and a thousand other welcoming things. But it soon died down though not before I had been drunk every night for a month on end.

I was usually put to bed about two in the morning to be called at midday with an orange and a brandy and soda. Lunch was my breakfast, taken alone and always fried sole and sausages because I thought that by not varying my food I was giving my stomach less to do. I felt extremely ill and every day went alone to a cinema after which I tried to write. The novel was almost finished and it became the last foothold to write just one more page a day, the last line of defence because I was miserable in fits and starts and felt insane.

The experience had this odd side to it. As I would walk along between these mouldering walls haunted by the tolling bell there was sure to be sounding out of the sky from one direction or another and which this was I could not tell, men often came up I felt certain I had never seen before. With my stomach in such a state I hardly knew if I was on this earth the stranger would say something like how are you this afternoon and would make some reference to a previous evening. I had been too drunk to remember him afterwards and sometimes on these occasions I wondered whether the man was real standing there as mumbled a reply. One horrible time a man like this I could not recall had a flake of stone on his shoulder. I fled. This was a short time of great degradation relieved by one piece of good fortune which lasted.

Whether it is that at school the masters make the boys or the boys, being as they are, make the masters the poor fish they almost always seem to be, it is safe to say that undergraduates make the dons. A don almost invariably begins by making friends for the first nine years of his time and then, when he has found three lots of friends drop out he begins to have had enough, he sees more of his fellow dons until after eighteen years he will see only his own pupils and, when he is off duty, none but his colleagues. It was my good luck to find two or three dons who were still so young that they were seeing undergraduates. We made them, if they will excuse this, because their work, being highly specialized in subjects such as the dead languages would, if they had been left to it while still in the thirties, have finally and completely dried them up. In return we had the benefit of minds drawn by their success not only from England but from throughout Europe into this repository Oxford is of everything intellectually the best and we should have been fools if we had not jumped at the chance that contact with such minds offered. For if we kept them alive by offering them relaxation they put life into us by the elixir it must be at twenty to find oneself measured up to anything so outstanding as this exceptional race of men.

The experience for those who have not had it can best be described by the picture of a traveller who has come some of the way and now finds himself bewildered, suspicious and rather tired because he has not found the sort of country he has been seeking, part of his difficulty being that he is not sure quite what climate or kind of scenery is necessary to his peace of mind. He comes to a place where the winding track he follows through nettles breaks into two and there above a great number of broken bottles are a profusion of signposts obviously false, giving details of the amenities offered by following the direction indicated. The day is hot, the way has been long, flies and wasps have been troublesome, and all the time there has been a persistent knelling in the distance to work up a feeling of foreboding.

Also the sense is strong that it will soon be too late. At the intersection of this track however he comes upon a tall gaunt figure dressed neatly as if for London but with something untidy about him, perhaps in the uneasy protuberance of his eyes. He appears to be resting without discomfort just off one of these paths with nettles about but it is plain that in his case they do not sting because he outstings them and there are no flies on him. He speaks first, in time he will ask the traveller to sit down, but for the present he is content to describe exactly where you want to go and just why what you want is so necessary. One is suspicious at first that he will conclude with an overpowering argument or even with proof that one is a fool to look for whatever it may be but, when the time comes for his conclusion, one finds with delight that he is in complete agreement and what is more that he has far more cogent reasons in one's favour than one has been able to produce. Nothing of what he says is put directly, a great deal of it is fireworks let off to conceal the trend of what in two years' time you may suspect to be towards sentiment, it is all hedged about by the steam power of this trained mind and in a rain of words. As your suspicion evaporates you discover these to to be tending towards your case and in the end justifying it perhaps with a sad but wonderful story of what befell someone who took the other road.

It is most comforting, so much so that when, as

will certainly happen sooner rather than later, he is to be heard brilliantly advocating exactly the reverse because what did for the one case may not do for another there is no sense of disillusionment, nor, quite rightly, that white can never be black, that is that two diametrically opposed arguments cannot be equally satisfactory, for he has it in him to take every side and to be nearly always right. You learn that you have been on the best road all along but you also find this fact must be accepted dispassionately, that your being in the right is no reason for anyone else being wrong.

This is what they taught me. I do not say they believed it nor that I gathered the whole point. It certainly does not follow that any of us believe it now. What is true is that it was just what was needed by one such as myself after the sort of school I had been to. Having taken it in there was no more need to have to fight to be an individual, to punch a way out of that stifling room filled with cotton wool. There were no obligations and the standards at last were those of the grown up world, namely ability and character. It was like getting out of prison and that is one reason why, like many another escaped prisoner, for a short while I took to drink.

The money snobbery was acute. Several undergraduates had incomes of up to three thousand pounds a year and they were sought after for their cars and the parties they gave. Without exception the rich of that generation were the most unpunctual people I have ever met. They behaved like stage favourites and when you were invited to a meal it was usual to be kept waiting three-quarters of an hour before the host, languid with money, deigned to come in.

There was also a realignment between those who had been at the same school at the same time. It by no means followed that past members of the prefects' club still went arm in arm about, some of them moved on to better things, some I was glad to see dropped out. For London and the great country houses were calling and a man one had been happy and safe to kick on his knee-cap where he stood by a corner every day at school to be so kicked because he enjoyed it, was taken up as they say. It did not follow that because his father was an enormously rich man he need yet be in receipt of a huge allowance, it was the potentiality of the vast wealth that one day should be his which made him an irresistible attraction. It mattered not at all that he was a charming man. In these circles ability and character counted for as little as they were to count in after years when women would come love-hunting money with the prestige they had acquired through being photographed in the weekly press and I only instance these acquaintanceships, while not questioning their importance, for the pleasure to be had out of seeing peculiarly repulsive members of that prefects' club fall back where they belonged, into the limbo of footballers not good enough to get a blue.

There were as many defections from the Society of Arts, not that any of us believed in art, but from the attitude we had adopted of non-cooperation. Realising, I suppose, that a drawing room is better than a garret because the same things can be done in both and the more comfortably in the first, several of us went after those whose character it was to be rich or whose ability stretched to the possession of a title and who am I to complain who had a lord for a near relation and a drawing room and a garret under the one roof at home. And indeed it is only when one looks at it in the light of imminent death, that rather ghastly colour in the sky of mustard yellows with the sirens wailing their call of now you may have to die that one begins to doubt whether everything really has been for the best. The bells chime the death of time which is always passing, but the sirens warn that there may be no more, that the watch may stop.

WE played at being gentlemen. For the first time we could order lunch to be served in our own rooms by going to the kitchens and talking through a hatch to the chef in his white cap. In the end, I do not know why, the main dish was always duck. Then we visited the Junior Common Room to choose wine with the head steward and this always turned out to be hock. Duck no doubt was what could most easily be cooked, and they had laid down a great store of hock. In this way we learned something you may not realise at once, that with the one cook there is likely to be the same food for guests, and the one wine from the same supplier. If you fight against this disaster may follow as when at the end of a meal at which I had not given them duck my best friend asked if there would be any chocolate because he had not had enough. There was no escape from what was thought right for a lunch party, but all the same all through the first year there seemed to be a choice of everything in the world with this extravagance of liberty we found.

Here we fingered long stemmed glasses and sniffed the wine, holding it up to the light which came through our narrow gothic-ridden windows. We spoke knowingly of vineyards with German names but had to be told when the wine was corked. A lunch party there, if it is to count as a success, should not disperse any earlier than four o'clock. Cigars have to be offered, port and brandy, and one never hears the host say afterwards of his guests that all went well only he had been unable to get rid of them. For we had leisure and everything was before us. Even if we played badly from inexperience this was the blessed time of summing up what we imagined we were to find when the world was to fall at our feet upon our entry. We talked forward from the particular to the general, whereas we are wise enough now after dinner when there are no women present to talk back, instancing the way friends have changed, of this marriage or the other, that did it, and always without generalizations.

It is wrong in the state the world is at the time this is written to assume that other generations have not had quite such forebodings about the immediate future. It may be unnecessary to be in such a hurry to write this book. What does at this moment seem pertinent is our attitude at that time. The war well won for us it appears we forgot those who had lost their lives and that we sat back like victors who had themselves successfully borne arms. It seems in a way as though we have been falsified by the turn events have taken. For my own part I know when

alone I spent some hours each day, now complacent-
ly, now with anguish, looking forward to falling in
love I did not know with whom and I question
whether this was quite enough.

Whether we were at fault or not we collected
Victorian objects, glass paperweights with coloured
posies cast in them, little eternalized baskets of
flowers which nothing could break, sometimes they
were in the stoppers of bottles, and large piles of
waxed fruits under high glass domes rarer because
they were the more fragile. A number of us bought
spotted dogs in china from Staffordshire, one or two
had figures of the Prince Consort in the same
material. As to architecture we were for everything
Gothic and Beckford was a writer much admired.
At the same time the last volumes of ' *A la Recherche
du Temps Perdu* ' were coming out and anyone who
pretended to care about good writing and who knew
French knew his Proust. Though I am not a Jew a
don compared me to Swann. This gave me great
pleasure but the character who never failed to be
mentioned not less than once each evening was
Charlus. In some reminiscences of an older man it is
written that the undergraduates of his day waited
for a new book by Kipling in an almost unendurable
suspense. If any contemporary of mine wants to
realise how painful it will be to grow old and
begin not to understand let him think of the time
when the undergraduate sitting back in the security

our deaths have bought, will treat Proust as we treated Kipling.

Those were the days of silent films when anyone with a hangover wept at words of his own he put onto the lips of the girl reproving her drunken lover on the screen, of Mary Pickford, " The World's Sweetheart," speechless yet or, for girls, of Valentino who never said a word in films. For me the darkness, that is the light subdued, the snivelling and soft laughs, those heads more intent on each other's breath as in the oldest gesture they inclined one to the other against the lighted screen the orchestra played low to, here was the place in which to work out the sense of guilt, to conquer that nausea of lunch after the night before's drinking. The days were a stupor until, in the evening with a few quick drinks, the mind was lit again by the daylight of whisky with friends, and after more hock, because we mixed our drinks, the old kaleidoscope reappeared of the fabulous relationships between people known to all of us with the spotlight of confidences; all this when Rome was perhaps already burning.

But here for the first time one was part of a life which is unperishing, for even if we had been sheltered by our lack of responsibilities my generation had been through a time of upheaval and had not in their homes or at their public schools known until joining the University a life they could be sure would continue. At Oxford, should everyone go up on a

scholarship and the one subject be engineering, it
will always be the first storm of fresh air for most
people, whatever their circumstances, the fan putting
its roar into the furnace. Here for hundreds of years
there has been the extravagance of youths coming
upon liberty they have never tasted yet which for
those who can afford idleness and for many who cannot is sufficient to shew how foolish they can be. And
those who go there to work find no restrictions on
burning candles only the loneliness long hours bring
deep into the night. These two extremes of behaviour
and the thousand ways of living in between, the
mixing of work and pleasure, gave a picture which
at last seemed to be an inkling of what we were so
soon to find when we in our turn joined the outside
world. In fact of course it was a caricature when we
thought it a work of art but it had been unchanging
through all the changes of the years. Later, for the
twenty-four months I worked through my father's
factory, and an account of this will close the book, I
was to find the most slowly altering life of all, skilled
manual labour. But here, in Oxford, from the com-
pulsion of his nature free at last to begin to express
itself was the extraordinarily magnified, pitiful,
shifting and amusing show of the moneyed man
offered up to life's tricks and surprises, valuable
because so much of man's time is spent in acquiring
the capital necessary to lead such a life of leisure,
though not on such a scale, or of work which he can

choose for himself. And with the dons, as in a kind of elysium, as nowhere else, and this was unique, here was a life in which ability and to a lesser degree character was the only criterion until they had reached middle age and for the best of them until they were dead.

Mixed up in this, because real life is an inextricable tangle, were social activities. Many undergraduates were claiming these as if by right for their life's work, and justified their having the money with which to afford them, as people always will, by picking upon some line like Victorian objects to make the link, the conversation at their meals. And I, who am too weaknatured to live without routine, having finished my novel and had it accepted, with nothing to do all day and dimly conscious of what I have just put down, thought I should go mad while beginning to know a sort of continuing happiness at last, in a place I knew would always be there but in which by the time I had found it I doubted whether I had a right to share. If there is a paradise there are many natures who will always worry whether they ought not to be somewhere else.

I had taken English as my school and that meant learning Anglo-Saxon. This I found I could not do and for the rest discovered that literature is not a subject to write essays about. We had to get off one of these a week, and if we were punctual we kept out of trouble with the tutors. I suppose I did not have to do more than six hours work in seven days.

I was haunted, as has been described, by a sense of insecurity and by a sense of importance now the novel was to be published. I could not believe that men earning three pounds a week for difficult work, which before I had met it I thought more difficult than it was, would tolerate the kind of life I led for, while my allowance was no more than anyone received who had been at my public school I managed to live at an altogether higher rate by sponging on richer friends. And that I should be an author, a thing I never thought I was while writing, seemed by the fact of what I wrote being accepted for publication to make me the only undergraduate member of an exclusive London club. Because, after the first flush of social success, I was no longer the most popular man of my year and was soon no more than one of many rather on the outskirts of a set.

There were consolations and they were more valuable than any sense of ease. With those of us who met in the dons' rooms, and there were among us men of every description although more or less of the same mind, there was no lack of that praise we had so missed at school but which we now dealt out to each other as and when required. For once we were with people who spoke the same language and now it was not so much a question of words as it had once been but of the ideas which informed them. At school one talked to startle, at Oxford to impress. Instead of being made to think one was a tiresome freak with whom it was trying to be in the same house one was surprised at first to find one's ideas, which of course were hackneyed enough, treated as the most natural in the world and extended beyond where one had stopped into something that was a mirage of what might be fact. We tried to throw up a separate but enlarged, a shimmering picture of one aspect of a friend's affairs which would be well enough done to carry conviction and for another to embroider. So that we, the once rejected, as we became more expert rose to a sense of our importance and knew we were at last accepted, athletic success being lost in the welter of athletes. There was a saturation of games players. And all the time I was there I did not know one member of the eleven by sight. Because the place was so much larger there were enough people to be found for any taste, there was a niche for everyone to occupy however small. But oddly enough it made for shyness.

To be convincing, to get the reason one put forward for a certain person's lack of success accepted was to hold a mirror up to facts as we wanted them, to create a flattering illusion. The reasons given became proof why this man would never do well and the cause of our holding this opinion of him would invariably be that he was not one of us. If you are not on our side at Oxford you are against us and that is why you are wrong. We played this patience with skill and it was heartening. It even followed us to London. But we were not a mutual admiration society because the strain it was to keep a level high enough to convince clever and sensitive men led to shyness.

I had never watched myself before when talking and the effort made me differently shy, that is I mercifully talked less. It had this effect even outside the dons' circle, I began to carry it when amongst those with whom I had been the man of my year and for years afterwards if with strangers in London I could not speak naturally.

At Oxford these two sets were on top of their spheres, that is each was best of its kind, the one in good talk and the other in high living. They were always meeting as their counterparts had at my first school. That friend who had been leader of the Society of Arts had asked the prefects club to his oyster tea and they had accepted. By no means every previous member of that club was now one of those who carried the spirit on in each other's rooms, their numbers were reinforced by *ex officio* members whose right their great homes gave them, we were so grown up by this time, to grace any exclusiveness of that kind. For our part we some of us held the entry to both worlds but our yardstick in the main was the opinion these younger dons, some of whom

were able snobs, held of our intelligence and con-
viviality. And as the best of two worlds will always
be meeting so we wined and dined each other.
Inasmuch as we did so we lived necessarily in a con-
tradiction. The two circles should not have met but
they do always everywhere and the life I led I felt
then I should not lead although I am not of that
opinion now.

One knew well enough that whatever happened
this life I have tried to describe would always continue at Oxford, even if the one set should be the sons
of commissars and the other brass finishers' children,
but we lived at a time when no one who remained
conscious could fail to ask himself whether it was the
life for him. At any rate, without holding any
political views, that is what drove me to go down in
a year's time, in 1927, to see for myself how by far
the greater number live in England. This move was
the easier because my living was to come out of the
factory I worked through. It was killing two birds
with one stone, which helped.

But it must not be assumed that because a number
of us bought Victorian relics we were a weakhearted
crew nor that, through being physically weak, we
compensated by exhibitionism. It is true we wore
roll top collar jumpers, suede shoes, and, when we
went to London, black hats all of which at that date
were abominations to some men and women. There
may have been occasions when we were very

frightened but on the whole we fought when we had to fight or at any rate put a good face on any ugly situation.

My room in college was across the landing to that of a well known athlete. A few days after I first arrived he came in to ask if I would play for one of the junior football teams and I had my lie ready, that I had a weak heart. He accepted this, commiserated with me and could not have found anything objectionable to his taste in my rooms. I hated then, as I do now, to have them elaborately decorated but the real reason was that if I had tried in deference to what pleased my friends to put up some unusual curtains these would have proved a waste of money. By knowing the people I did the hearties in college would almost inevitably have wrecked them. The days of feather pictures were past and of horse sunbonnets. At school and at Oxford one did things to startle, one now takes no unavoidable step.

We were in a rougher world. After life at school it was hard to believe the authorities could encourage orgies like Bump suppers for the rowing men and their supporters, that is ninety-five out of every hundred in the college. Of course they were right but it did seem to turn the rest of us into early Christians for a Roman holiday. We were not poison to them because we could be thought bad for the school, that is the college, but it was because there were so few of us that we were fair game.

On evenings such as these one took care to get
drunk so that, if they did come it would not hurt too
much, and also to stay out of college as late as
possible. The most that was likely to happen was
that they would drop one into the Cherwell from a
bridge but they were so mad drunk always on these
nights that I felt there was a chance they might do
me serious injury. On the other hand the door to
each undergraduate's room had an outer door which
could be bolted after which it was impossible for any
number of them to open it from the outside or to
break it down. One had only to close this to be safe
from the whole University. I never did because I
thought if they came and could not get at me they
would lie in wait to take me another day, and that
the suspense I should be in of waiting would not be
worth while.

The first Bump supper was the worst. It was held
while my popularity was still great with my friends.
They were fearless and thought it would be amusing
to have a party in my rooms that very night and fight
heavily outnumbered if fight they must. I did not
like the idea but was awkwardly placed. If I
refused to have the party my friends would think
me a coward, and if I had it I should be a
marked man in college. In the event the hearties
never went for me after this party but whether it
was that they respected defiance or that they
feared to do me injury because I was already

playing billiards for the University no one will ever know.

We had our party and they had theirs. Visitors had to be out of the college by midnight and about eleven a really howling mob appeared on my staircase which was also that of the famous athlete. I was drunk and cannot remember this too well but had the sense to get a dozen bottles half full of beer and fill them up with brandy. These we passed to those rowing men slavering in the doorway, they took a pull and passed them back to the dervishes behind and soon they went away to become unconscious. They had been drinking port all night, the beer and brandy on top was too much for any stomach.

On any other Bump supper evening, when I got back just before the gate into College was closed, there was the difficulty of reaching my rooms unseen and then the wait far into the night with every now and then a rush of them through the cloisters, that awful screaming they affected when in motion imitating the cry when the fox is viewed, that sense curiously of remorse which comes over one who thinks he is to be hunted, the regret, despair and feeling sick the coward has.

This would be the point to put in a story of how brave I have been once, if done with enough modesty it would look well here. Unfortunately there is worse to follow, but after two more stories there will be nothing else of the kind. At school, during a general election, the friends I was later to join at Oxford had gone out to a nearby town to hold a meeting. They were conservatives then, they were socialists most of them at the University, and now a number are a sort of conservative again. They took me along, we became separated and they got into the middle of a crowd which began to use threats. They were pushing their way through for home and I and another were at a distance in front making off in the same direction. We did not know if they wanted help, it certainly looked like it. We excused our not going back by saying to each other that if they had been such fools as to get into trouble with the crowd they could get themselves out. But we were looking over our shoulders as we went further and further in front. It was at this moment a small ragged working man we had not noticed said: " Would they be friends of yours in there ? " With a strong sense of guilt we admitted it. " Well then " he said " my lads you go back to your pals what is in trouble," and we went back, ashamed.

Now at Oxford we had formed a railway club because one of us knew by heart whole tracts of Bradshaw. Once in each term we hired a restaurant car attached to an outgoing train and had dinner on it until the time came to be uncoupled and sent back by another. We drank a great deal on these trips and wore dinner jackets. That is dressing to startle.   On one occasion the train our car was attached to on the way back carried a university hockey team and several thick ankled supporters. They saw us on the platform before we were turned round and, perhaps because we were having so much more of a time than themselves, once the journey began they enticed one of us into their coach and beat him up.   I believe he fought alone against eighteen of them before they knocked him out.   I shall always be sorry I had not the courage to be in the rescue party when we missed him.   They did not have to fight, they found the hockey team in tears at what they had done, the ridiculous lionhearted apes they were.

Things happened that one has seen comedians do in films.   Towards the end of my time at Oxford there was another Bump supper which, although I did not attend, I thought I should try out sober. Early in the morning, in strong moonlight that projected the Gothic arches which lined the cloisters down like a maze over the stone pavement, I was hurrying with a bottle of Eno's to the one friend I had in College, my footsteps falling with a moonlit sound on the chalk flags, the traceries traced out so deep that I stretched to step over their shadows and the sky seen through the outlines above extruded by the moon a killed blue, the stars the stunned light. I heard first and then I saw three figures coming, the maze crawling over them as they moved and I made out it was two men supporting a third. His head lolled as though his throat were cut but when he heard me he pulled it up by one hair-entangled hand and how he managed in his condition I do not know but he saw the bottle in my arms and it meant drink to him. He broke loose, ran forward and after a struggle he snatched it away. He let his head go and this time it fell back and then he poured the powder down his throat. At once he fell on his back face upwards in a moonlit diamond and began silverly frothing. We laughed until we choked as he was choking. The bubbles came out of his mouth in a growing moon froth mound as though each were an animal which, to get warm, would cover his face and, lo, soon they had put their air light bodies on his eyes. Then he got up sober and went unaided to his rooms.

Again, on almost every night one term a friend would dress up as an old lady to go down to the club after dinner. He wore a Victorian costume of course with a huge red wig and thick veil. The streets were not well lighted and with terrible obscene gestures he wavered down the road ahead half seen half lost as following him we laughed and laughed like bullies in a German film. And it was in rooms when living out of college that the friend I shared these with and I had our first girl to lunch. I believe she had not been alone to an undergraduate's sitting room before and when she came wearing a fur round her shoulders and he went up behind in what he thought was old-fashioned courtesy to help her off with it, she shrieked and then cried out " whatever are you doing ? "

THESE were now the days of Hunt Balls. You pay to go, or are paid for, and they are held in aid of the Hunt which, however fashionable, is always in need of money. They take place after a Committee of the most powerful followers has quarrelled over what shall be offered for the money charged; year after year at home a number would call for an oyster bar to replace something, I have forgotten what, they thought the evening could do without. These quarrels, which are invariable, are known to all and on the night they do not make the fun any greater except for those who like myself go to stir up a little trouble. Indeed there can hardly be any who look forward to a function of this kind except perhaps a few very young girls who have no other chance to meet fresh men.

In our family we were drawn into, but took no part in, the rows which preceded the so-called Ball. Our difficulty was not so much to persuade others how it should be arranged as it was to get a party together. This was never easy, we liked to think because of the distance from London, and in order to make the numbers even it was necessary, after the girls and men we wanted to have most had some of them refused, to ask others we would rather have done without. This would mean we seldom looked forward to the night and it goes without saying that the girls who stayed with us must have been more bored than ourselves if only because they were made to have so many more of these exaggerated parties.

For a son there is a fatal ring to the words " Her mother was an old friend of mine," and the reverse must be true for girls when they hear their mothers say, " His father was one of my dancing partners." At the same time there is no alternative, short of co-educational schools there is nothing for it at first but to make the best of those of the opposite sex produced by one's parents and their friends from the time when they themselves were young and when they, as we were soon to be, were having their first children.

As I write this at the Beach, which is a swimming-pool open to the sky at Monte Carlo, two little boys are playing with a little girl. They are just old enough to run without falling. The game is for these boys to smother the girl with kisses so that with having them all over her she is drowning in so far as she cannot breathe. She loves it and when they run away, screaming, to tease her and annoy us, she gets up and toddles after, wanting more.

All that and more it seems is open to the French so soon. But when, at one of our house-parties, a man staying with us told one of his partners that her hair smelled good, there was a hullaballoo. She told the other girls we had asked to meet him, and who am I to see into their minds or the feelings which at that time did duty for their intelligence but they made him an apple-pie bed and set a booby trap with his chamber pot all because he had said this. Is it any wonder I was shy with girls ?

It must be a question of the sun. These Balls are held in the Town Hall of the nearest county town and the drive out after dinner was no spin to get cool after the long day's sun as once some years later at Vera Cruz we used to ride in an open tram to get a little air down our throats. It was a case of wrapping up, the rain on these nights came pouring down so that to get into a motor the women had to risk their shoes. Then when we had at last arrived there were no stars, as in the song, up above, but in the blackness of the night outside the earth was covered under steady rain unseen by us, the cattle in lost fields with their flanks smoking at any break in the weather and a damp cold blanketing all these unused rooms opened this evening for the Ball.

At one of these affairs I was dancing with a hideous girl and said to break new ground, " I like the chandelier," and she said, " How nice for the room."

It must be the lack of sun for who can make conversation next day over Irish stew at a shooting-lunch in one of the cottages on the estate, rain still drumming, everyone wet and also soaked in what is left to them of the night before, the band, the worse champagne, and only on such occasions the stale quails in aspic the Committee ordered because they had always had them because they sounded good.

At every Hunt Ball I have ever gone to there has been a balcony overlooking the floor and this is where I try to spend the evening. Once for one dance they turned a few lights out and played it low. There were two girls sitting by and one said, " Isn't the music sad, it makes me want to sob." She meant it by the tone of her lisp, she misty as our elms through August but caught now by the bitter draughty cold I sat in trying to hear more of what they murmured through their blood.

The Hunt Ball is always on a Friday night. The guests stay over the week-end. It is difficult to know what to do with them in the evenings. Sometimes we used to play sardines, of all games the most simple and pathetic in that one couple can never stay long alone. The rules are that a man and a woman hide and the rest hunt in pairs throughout the house. When the first to hide are found the two who discover them have to crowd into the same hiding-place and so on, more and more pile in, it may be under a big bed, until there is one couple left still looking and they have lost. Lost what ? Why the game.

For another amusement every light in the house had to be turned out. One of the downstairs rooms was called a sanctuary and the party was split into two sides. One side, less numerous, had to catch the others as separately or more often in pairs they crept through the dark to get into this room where they would be safe under the rules.

We had a game we invented for ourselves. In the cellars we caught spiders, marked a circle out on a table, divided the circumference into segments and putting the spider down in the middle betted on which spot it would cross the circle. Part of the fun was the way the girls screamed as these spiders made to drop off the table onto their laps and it was exciting to catch them in such a way that they were not injured and could run again. But the spiders were too wise and after they had been used twice would play no more, they crouched down where we put them and would make no move. We had then to get fresh ones and the game always ended in this way, that it was too much trouble to hunt more up again.

The only explanation is there was so little sun. The time of year in which we can expect some hours of it is when hunting and shooting ends. Then " everyone " went up to London to dance, sitting out on balconies to be fouled by petrol fumes, when only for those short months they could have shared the companionship good weather brings in the country, the light which is so beautiful when it settles on the colours of the fields in England but glaring in a town, impersonal. It is the men's fault that the sort of people I was brought up with reversed the seasons, stayed in London while the country was at its best and went back to the country when the climate was as bad as can be found in any civilized land. They would say there was no way out, that foxes must breed and pheasants lay eggs, that while this was going on and they could not shoot or hunt there was no point in not being in town. But the weather lies at the root of the way women and men behave, not so much this week's rain or that but over a period of years, and it seems the English in their relations with each other are less frank than other nationalities by the extent to which their skies are less clear and so by the less amount of sun they have.

I have always disliked being abroad for more than a fortnight but at the same time have often felt a stranger in England and the more so at that date because I had not found the sort of English life I liked. At the age I was then this was intensified by the false pride I took in having a book published. My attitude when away from my own friends was of non-cooperation softened when girls were about into fewer bursts of self-confidences which I wanted to be revelations. But I did not have the courage to be frank or perhaps we all of us had not had enough sun.

My friends and I were intolerant but by reason of it we lived in an integrity greater than most of us can claim today. One could be genuine at Oxford. Life is a succession of compromises and although we did not know it yet we had not begun to live. Better to refuse to dance as I did then and at the same time do the polite by sitting out with any one of our party who had no partner than as later to dance only with one or two and be superior while joining in even to the point of making the hunting person's jokes. Better, and I suppose this is very English, not to enjoy oneself at all than to overdo it as when only the other day I went to a Hunt Ball. Foxes are known as Charleys and so in some circles are women's breasts. I made some joke about how many people went after Charleys. It had a sort of success but was one of those things about oneself to be sorry for. And in those days, champagne or no, I would never have said it, or is it prim to admit that ?

As undergraduates we did not have to make terms, we could choose the people we saw and what is more we could to a certain extent control the persons seen by our friends through the exercise of malice. This would be true of London today if marriage had not entered into it, a friend's wife has her own companions and women as a rule have no idea how to be exclusive. Love, necessarily inclusive, is their interest for they want to bring everyone in. You understand we lived the life of a school of French painters and writers who see no one who is not one of themselves. That is my companions did but I kept my feet as far as possible in two camps. And it is not that one longs for such days to come back, and very far from the fact that I think those days were best, but this is a time to pay tribute and to settle old scores and what I am trying to express by implication is the real gratitude I have to Oxford.

On the 26th we leave Monte Carlo because I have a Board Meeting in London on the 28th. The next day I have to go to Blackpool, our works are having their outing. It is six hours from London so I get there late on Friday evening and, as they do not start back to Birmingham before ten on the Saturday night, I sleep in the place and start home on Sunday. Every year the men vote where they want to go and two or three years back they chose this town again. When I arrived on the Friday I went to the Tower and, as is the convention, asked one of the girls sitting about if she would dance. She got up without a word. She was pretty and well dressed so that it was unexpected to find her right hand had corns, was hard from her work. I made conversation. I said it was a marvellous floor, a wonderful band, a great place. She did not reply. So then I said I had never been before, had she ? and still she said nothing. So it went on and she did not speak until the number ended when all she brought out was, as she turned away, " no more, no more."

This is what I mean by Oxford. It is the wink when another friend is present so much as to say we can let this pass. I had not been speaking to the girl in her language whatever that may have been and she kept her attitude by not replying. She might have answered and carried my remarks to absurdity by agreeing too much, by taking these simplicities further even to saying " yes, I always think this floor divine, don't you ? " But she was content, as I had begun to learn to be as an undergraduate, just to disagree without saying so, perhaps to despise, but in any case she was self-confident enough to let it go and thus, if only by silence, to be as mysterious as our lack of sun demands, and that is, so far as most of us are concerned, to make herself real.

At school it had all been gabble but at Oxford after a time if you knew where to look there was to be found an informed silence which could be expressed. This is a kind of passionate self-confidence in a cause and which between friends can break into speech, it is not being superior even if it is being too sure, it is not joining in while still being an observant part, it is to point the way by indirect assertions as well as by silence, love, or as they would say there, passion can induce it, it is one of the happiest of all conditions within the reach of man.

The philosopher Bradley when out one day was introduced by a colleague to one who had just become a don. He asked what this man taught and was told he took pupils in logic. Bradley then had the humility to say, " I should not know where to begin."

But the General Strike came in my second year. No one will suppose with the attitude I thought I had won that I could take a hand. The moment it happened, striking just where I had been most afraid as for some time I had been unable to look a labourer in the eye, I had to get away at once. Within three days I had learned that where this attitude lets one down is on those rare occasions when we are all caught up into action, it is then that non-cooperation or the keeping silent becomes a cross.

My excuse to get away was ready. My parents were both in Mexico again, my brother was abroad so I asked leave to go to look after our house in the country and was one of the first to get out of Oxford.

I hired a car. The strawberries were ripening at home and I thought I should be able to eat them in peace. But on the drive home we had to pass through Reading and in that town at a crossroads was a crowd of about three thousand people watching a policeman with no traffic to direct. His face was white because they did not make a sound, no one so much as coughed in this unnatural silence of the strike, they only stared at him. We stopped, wondering if it would be safe to go by and that is why I know it was so quiet with their waiting, as I felt, for one man to throw a stone when all would have joined in. And was it their comment in bitterness at things as they found them or was it curiosity this silence that seemed on the surface to be so like the attitude I had adopted and which I thought then to be unique to my sort of education ?

There was a knell in this experience for ears attuned to Oxford bells and to mutterings of a life I did not know but feared. It was the crowd's silence which drove the point home and a day or two later it was an old man's voice over the telephone, a neighbour, who asked a question that has been echoed in these last few months and, likely enough, will only too soon be heard loud voiced again.

I had been eating the strawberries when I was told this man was asking for me. I had forebodings as I went to answer. He wanted to know what my plans were in the emergency. Here all pretence at non-cooperation failed. I said I would do any kind of " national " work. " Well done my boy well done," he cried, using those immemorial words.

He sent me to unload bananas at Avonmouth and as it happened when I got there they thought I was running away from home. Because he had muddled my credentials I was not allowed on the ship.

One is always caught up, one inevitably has to take a hand but what I miss now is the reluctance I had then. It is not that one was ever afraid to die. One may resent being killed, but most of us are quite ready. What is despairing in my case is that I should acquiesce, in the old days I should never have done so, and that is my farewell to youth in this absolute bewilderment of July 1939, that I should be so little unwilling to fight and yet likely enough to die by fighting for something which, as I am now, for the life of me I cannot understand.

But I was soon to leave Oxford for good. The Hunt Balls, the shooting, even my billiards, the intolerance, the ability to keep silent just learned, the convictions and these last above all, all were to be left behind; nothing was ever so easy again, we were never to be so sure of anything afterwards. I was never to have so much time to myself and what I was to have would be after a day's work in the factory or office. Being tired in the head was to be the brilliant fruit of my labours in the day to sour the evenings. But there were advantages.

The moment I left Oxford to go to Birmingham was the bridge from what had been into what is so much a part of my life now that a great deal is indistinguishable through being so close, too near to put down but more than that, it was an introduction to indisputable facts at last, to a life bare of almost everything except essentials and so less confusing, to a new world which was the oldest.

That is to say that I lived in lodgings, worked a forty-eight hour week first in the stores, then as a pattern maker, then in the ironfoundry, in the brass-foundry and finally as a coppersmith, and wrote at night. Week in week out I averaged eleven hours a day, so that I was only a visitor, I hardly took part at all in the life outside the " shop." I had to sleep nine hours at night, five days a week we worked eight and a half hours each day, lunch was an hour on top of that, getting to work and back and having supper took another hour, then I averaged two and a half hours writing, and this left only two hours to fiddle about in. My time was so full it went so fast I had no chance to do more than simplify everything.

On Saturday afternoons I went to see the Villa play, then on to a cinema and after a huge supper and a lot to drink I went to bed. On Sundays I almost always worked right through the day. This was to make up for doing no work for years, with my hands or my head but only with my feelings. So that when I say I found the life satisfying and I had never before been satisfied, the long hours of being occupied may have coloured what I thought I saw so that it may only be, but surely this is more than just something, that the life was happy.

There is nothing like work to make the time go and this at regular hours governed by a whistle leads to the remark so often heard in a factory as to how time flies. Again, it may have hurried in my case because I knew I was not to be there long, also perhaps because I had been so afraid of this life I was now to find more than bearable. The men themselves, the few that bothered to think about it, were of the opinion I had been sent there to be punished. They can take it from me theirs is one of the best ways to live provided that one has never been spoiled by moneyed leisure which is not as they would put it, something better.

Ours was the sort of place with very little repetition work. We employ highly skilled men most of whom have been with us for years. At the time I went there when hardly anyone had more than a crystal set, the announcers of the B.B.C. had not got going with their B.B.C. English so that I sometimes had trouble to make my accent understood or to understand theirs. But everyone was kind as I began to learn how little money means except security and how little literature counts, that overblown trumpet, when leisure is so restricted. That is I write books but I am not proud of this any more than anyone is of their nails growing, and if it be argued that I was happier at this period because I had less free time than most you will be wrong, almost everyone of the age I had reached who was not a labourer went to night school to learn more of whatever trade he was in.

Moneyed people have invented interests to pass their long hours of leisure and whatever their inclinations, that is whether they are interested or not they read, they look at pictures and listen to music. They become constipated with things they cannot grasp. In the ironfoundry we had a close discussion each day in the lunch hour nearly always about some non-political event in the news. At least once in every week we discussed where a certain Stony Lane had been, which, soon after the war, had been obliterated in a clearance scheme in the district. No one agreed about its exact position nor whether a path with a stile had been one way of getting into it from another row of houses the name of which escapes me. This was a regular turn but the point I am trying to make is that the conversation was more like that of intellectuals than the half-baked talk about novels people who fancy themselves put over. An odd thing was that many of the Socialists in our works read Conservative daily papers because they thought the news service better. It is papers like the *Daily Express* which specialize in extraordinary human events that sell best. We had between half-past twelve and half-past one an exclusive interest in the evidence each day brought of how someone or other had behaved in the sort of crazy situations forty million people living on an island can produce. We were not alone in this of course, but I had not yet met, and have not since, such concentration on human behaviour. This did not extend to curiosity about one another's circumstances, anything approaching what is known as gossip was never tolerated.

People are inclined to dismiss too airily the big difference money makes in the amount of security their money gives them. On three or four pounds a week life can be comfortable so long as the family is in good heath, but what margin there is cannot cover protracted illness. That and the question of whether he can keep in work are the two great worries of the artisan, but this last does not bother him too much, if he knows his trade he can get another job except during one of the comparatively rare cycles of bad trade. As against this he need not think overmuch about his work while at it, and when he knocks off for the day he has no reason to think of it again until the next morning. On top of that there is the deep, the real satisfaction of making something with his hands. This has to be experienced to be believed, it is more than sensual and is obviously the purest form of self-expression. But the lack of security that illness or unemployment brings does lead to an almost cryptic dismissal of a fellow worker's personal affairs which, amusingly enough, is very near the public school spirit, however different the cause.

It would be unfair to say the works suited me better than anything had done for years because I had been an idler who had at last found something to occupy his mind and hands. It would be equally absurd to say that, if these men had had the time to take up books, they would have been better able to stand reading than those whose excess of leisure or whose boredom had driven them to it. On the contrary they will make bad readers when, if we are not to have a war and hours are to get shorter, they will be pitchforked into it if their gardens are not made very much larger. One and all are violently opinionated, it is not lack of education, I do not know what it is, and reading does surely require an open mind. They are like Americans, they may say they agree but they never listen, and this is one reason why they express themselves with an unheard of clarity. And their speech, unadulterated by literature as it is and unaffected when I was there by the B.B.C. has something which is much more than clearness. When they describe, as everyone knows, they are literally unsurpassed in the spoken word, as in the following:

" His eyes started out of his head like little dog's testicles."

A labourer on his brown dog:

" What he likes is I take him out into the fields week-ends and he rolls 'im white in the grass."

Or:

" In the trenches, in the War, before they were going over the top they had an issue of rum, see, but one of the chaps felt a bit queer and put his down on the parapet because he reckoned he'd bring it up if he swallowed it. And a big rat come along and drank it down, then sits up and says, ' now for the cat '."

And this is a story of great hilarity, the best of all, told with a hyphen in the middle of the word beautiful so as to pronounce it be-eautiful.

" A cow in a field saw a beautiful buttercup but when she sat down to eat this beautiful buttercup she found a bee had settled on it and the cow said to the bee you get off, this is my beautiful buttercup but the bee said I will not I got here first. So the cow said you go on get off it and the bee said I will not and the cow said I saw it first but the bee said I was here in front of you, so then the cow said if you don't I shall eat you as well as my buttercup but the bee said if you do I will sting you after. Then the cow ate the beautiful buttercup and the bee and when the bee was down in the cow's belly he thought it all was so dark so nice and warm he might as well have a nap before he stings the cow. So he drops off for a bit but when he woke up the cow was gone."

And this is a story from Oxford. The difference sufficiently underlines the distance between these two dissimilar worlds.

" In the war, without saying a word to anyone, the Professor of Arabic at one of the universities took ship to Arabia and, as soon as he had landed, journeyed into the interior not to Mecca or any other forbidden city but to a town out of touch with Europeans. Once there no news could be had of him and in due course the authorities decided they would send two officers and some men to make enquiries. This party set out and after travelling seven days they came to some palms which gave the first shade they had had and which marked the outskirts of the oasis the Professor had chosen. They rested beside their camels and stopped an Arab. They asked whether the Professor was in the town they could see from where they were sitting and were told he was. They wanted to know what he did all day and the answer was that in the mornings he lectured in modern Arabic and in the evenings in ancient Arabic. Rather at a loss they asked this man if the Professor's Arabic was good and he replied, ' His modern Arabic is good but his ancient Arabic is like attar of roses.' "

In putting my point this way I am of course confusing conversation with stories written here but meant to be told aloud which, when so told, escape the deadening effect print has so that anything in manuscript is more lively than the selfsame words whatever they may be after having been set in type at the printers. Again, through being accustomed to stories about Professors of Arabic one may not rise at them in quite the style as to the animal stories current in Birmingham when I was there and which, one must suppose, would with familiarity grow as tedious as any other sort of tale with a sort of meaning. But what people laugh about, not what they laugh at, is an indication of what they are like and the contrast between the different kinds of stories, not the dirty ones, that is, which are everywhere the same, may be the shortest way to point the difference.

This difference as I have tried to shew is largely occasioned by money, in other words it is accidental. In consequence those who must earn their living by manual labour are often much fitter physically than those who get their daily bread by the accident of sitting on an office stool. And this fitness leads directly to the gaiety there is in every well-run factory, the laughs, and there are plenty of them, when tears run freely and one has to sit down. When I was working in the coppershop I was mate to a man when we were given a large number of two-inch copper pipes to bend. We were sent off to another building which we had to ourselves and the first thing we had to do was, from the sketches, to draw out on the floor in chalk and in full scale the many different shapes we had to give these mains as they were called. We got in a muddle and I laughed more for a whole week with that man on that job than I have before or since, and real laughter is not so usual that one can dismiss the memory as of no consequence.

The gayest of all were the oldest labourers. Why this should be so I have no idea. It may be that their families had grown up so that the struggle to raise them was over at last, but most likely they had got into that blessed state when you forever cease to give a damn. Their obscenity, always in the form of comment or shouted advice was superb, beyond imagination magnificent. They had their off days but fewer than anyone else and some of the things they said, unprintable of course, will warm me always. If one should come to think of it at the end they would be worth dying for by those heroic comparisons in simple words so well chosen and arranged, so direct a communication they made one silly with laughing.

Why is it the French never seem to complain of their livers ? Is it that we are liverish through not having enough sun ? This state of health may be a delusion as much as the gaiety I thought I had found. For I was beginning to fall in love through the medium of a long exchange of letters and the manual work I did made me so well I thought as I walked through the morning dark to the factory in some way as though the pavements were no more than a part of what we breathe, no more that is than air and what goes to make it up. At that time one trod on open sky under the light of the infrequent lamps. Going home it would be dark again and I would be tired. But after no more than thirty minutes in a chair I was ready for hard work again.

But more than the escape out of being a schoolboy or an undergraduate, more than great good health, not as much as the company the day's work passed in but part of all this and arising out of it was the new standard which I had never met, that of costs and prices. The making something for little enough money that it would sell with the organization built up by my father in this factory to turn out what could be sold and then the other organization he presided over to sell what the factory could make, all this made sense and makes sense still. It was not hunting when it was no fun, not having to go shooting, it was not having to be polite to masters who were fools, it was to lose convictions, at a blow it was life itself at last in loneliness certainly at first, but, in that long exchange of letters then beginning and for the ten years now we have not had to write because we are man and wife, there was love.

LONDON. 1938/39.